Peace on Earth

Peace on Earth

Roots and Practices from Luke's Gospel

Joseph Grassi

LITURGICAL PRESS
Collegeville, Minnesota

www.litpress.org

Cover design by Ann Blattner. Illustration: Detail of *Initial E with Christ Sending Out the Apostles* from an Italian antiphonary, 15th century.

1   2   3   4   5   6   7   8

Library of Congress Cataloging-in-Publication Data

Grassi, Joseph A.
    Peace on earth : roots and practices from Luke's Gospel /
    Joseph Grassi.
        p. cm.
    Includes bibliographical references and index.
    ISBN 0-8146-2979-2 (alk. paper)
        1. Peace—Biblical teaching. 2. Peace—Religious aspects—
    Christianity. 3. Bible N.T. Luke—Criticism, interpretation, etc.
    I. Title.

BS680.P4G73 2004
226.4'06—dc22
                                                        2003058227

To Carolyn, my wife.
Her dedication to peace in her activism,
her poetry writings, and our family
have been a real inspiration.

Contents

Introduction

"PEACE ON EARTH," THE ANGELS' MESSAGE AT JESUS' BIRTH HAD A different meaning for Caesar and the Roman Empire. Peace and security were the highest priorities in the Empire and the basis of the *Pax Romana*. This peace was maintained by the Roman military, the most powerful force ever seen in the Western world. The purpose was economic, to maintain a steady flow of wealth to Rome and to keep the roads clear and safe for trade and business. There was no place for individual rights. Any disagreement with Rome was quickly punished often by the most severe and disgraceful means ever known, a most painful execution on the cross. Dissenters were quickly labeled as evil-doers and the equivalent of terrorists.

A central theme of Luke's Gospel is that announced by the angels at Jesus' birth: "Peace on Earth." As Luke presents it through Jesus, this theme is revolutionary and subversive, literally "turning the world upside-down." It is in direct opposition to the means used by the great world empires then as well as now. Their approach relies on power and force embracing a military solution to maintain an external mirage of peace. In contrast, Jesus, as a model for believers, teaches true peace through the practice of nonviolence, love, compassionate justice, true repentance, and forgiveness. External power and domination are renounced and replaced by inner power, humble service, and a priority for the needs of the poor and marginalized.

This approach however is far from being merely passive in the face of evil. Jesus also declares, "Do you think that I have come to bring peace on earth? No, I tell you but division" (12:51). Here Jesus refers to the false and deceptive "peace on earth" that results from passivity and acceptance. In contrast, strong stands on values and commitment must be made even at the serious risk of life and reputation.

This book will trace the theme of peace through Luke's Gospel, emphasizing the very practical means Jesus suggests to make it a reality. It will also focus on the inner empowerment available for all who wish to make true peace a priority in their own life and in the world of today.

1

"Peace on Earth"
Luke's Subversive
Christmas Story

"IN THOSE DAYS A DECREE WENT OUT FROM CAESAR AUGUSTUS THAT all the world should be registered" (2:1). As a child, I was deeply impressed by these words. So, at school, when I was asked to select a confirmation middle name, I chose "Augustus" so I could be the proud bearer of that awesome name. Now I smile to myself, as Luke must have done, as he described the divine contrasts in the story of Jesus' birth. Luke's story is "subversive" in the root meaning of "turning the world upside-down." This is the expression of Luke himself as used in Acts 17:6, where he describes the reaction of city authorities to Paul and Silas.

PAX ROMANA AND "PEACE ON EARTH"

Caesar's ostensible purpose for the census was to establish "peace on earth." This Caesar was Octavian (27 B.C. to A.D. 14) the first Roman Emperor after Julius Caesar. The centuries of "peace" that followed him were sometimes called *Pax Octaviana*, *Pax Augustiana*, or sometimes just *Pax Romana*. For Caesar and the Roman governors this meant no disturbances, rebellions, or threats to the Roman power needed to maintain the steady flow of money and goods to Rome from all over the world.

1

Pax Romana was enforced and guaranteed by the most powerful military machine the ancient world had ever known. The stone-paved Roman roads, some still in use, provided access to the military and to commerce all over the empire. Business was safe from bandits and attacks on land or from pirates at sea. Slave trade could continue until almost half the population of Roman cities were slaves. Money from taxes whether on individuals or goods poured into Rome from all over the world. There was no attempt to build up local economies unless this meant more Roman revenue.

To maintain "peace and security" any dissension was quickly squelched. Crime was often punished by a cruel and quick execution without a hearing. Few second chances were ever given. There was no popular voting, opportunity for discussion, or organized opposition to the invincible Roman armies. This meant that any dissension was expressed by bands of freedom fighters or "terrorists" who often had to rely on robbery and extortion to support themselves. They were generally a minority that was much feared by the general populace. Romans of this era made use of this atmosphere of fear by posing as saviors, keeping people from chaos by promoting Roman law, order, and security.

CAESAR, THE "DIVINE PEACEMAKER"

The Romans claimed divine authority for their role as "peacemakers." The senate gave Octavian the title of "Augustus" meaning "venerable" or worthy of worship. In the gospel story of tribute to Caesar (Mark 12:13-17), the coin of tribute had an image of the later Tiberius Caesar. There is a divine aura around his head, and the coin reads, "Tiberius Caesar, son of the divine Augustus." Octavian was the first Caesar after Julius. The latter was deified by the senate only a few months after his death in 42 B.C. The same honors were given to most other emperors, some of them even in their own lifetimes. Octavian built an altar of peace *(Ara Pacis)* in the Roman forum, where sacrifices and prayers were offered for peace. Later, he and most other emperors were appointed as *Pontifex Maximus*, supreme high priest, over Roman religion. Thus Roman emperors posed as divine warriors and peacemakers, promoting a holy war against all evildoers, opposition movements, and terrorists.

LUKE'S PURPOSE IN THE STORY OF JESUS' BIRTH

A central purpose of Luke is to proclaim Jesus' mission to establish a real inner peace from God rather than the pseudo-peace of *Pax Romana*. This inner peace is the fruit of a hidden plan of God that Luke expresses in his introductory gospel dedication to a certain "Theophilus." There Luke states his object to write about "the events fulfilled among us" (1:1). This fulfillment concerns the hidden plan of God that Luke plans to reveal in his Gospel. This inner plan contradicts the external plan of government authorities. Luke will show that this hidden plan is the "power of the Holy Spirit" behind human events rather than the power of earthly military prowess. We will illustrate this contrast in the selected areas or themes that follow.

THE CENSUS OF THE WHOLE WORLD
VERSUS THE POWER OF A CHILD AND LITTLE ONES

By way of contrasting God's hidden plan: On the outer human side, Caesar Augustus sends out a decree, *dogma*, to register the whole world to establish his absolute control. In the Roman world there was nothing so powerful as a *dogma* from the emperor. *But in the divine inner plan: God foils Caesar by making that decree an instrument to fulfill the prophecy that a great ruler will come from Bethlehem according to the prophecy of Micah 5:2,* "From you [Bethlehem] shall come forth for me one who is to rule in Israel." In Matthew's Gospel the prophecy is more explicit as the Magi come to Jerusalem and ask, "Where is the newly-born king of the Jews" (2:4). In response the Magi are directed to Bethlehem according to the prophecy of Micah.

To implement the *Pax Romana,* money from taxes and conscription of soldiers were urgently needed. The enforced registration and I.D. of each person were necessary tools to make this possible. The main Roman taxes were a poll tax on each individual as well as on land, produce, and business. To protest such censuses, there were frequent bitter tax revolts. The Acts of the Apostles mentions one of these under Judas the Galilean around the time of Jesus' birth (5:37). The Romans thoroughly crushed this uprising, punishing thousands of the Jewish freedom fighters with crucifixion, the cruelest and most shameful execution in the ancient world. In this atmosphere of terror, Joseph and his expectant wife Mary made the long and arduous journey from Nazareth to Bethlehem where they were expected to register.

In contrast to the grandiose plans of Caesar Augustus and his mighty army, God works in a humble way through little ones. Mary gives birth to her firstborn child and lays him in a manger because there is no room for them at the inn (2:7). The divine child is the exemplar for every child of God, as a "little one." The animals in their makeshift shelter provide hospitality. The only welcome committee is composed of shepherds who had been watching over their flocks nearby. In Jesus' own language, a little child was often called a "lamb," *talitha,* Aramaic, as Jesus calls the little girl he raised from the dead in Mark 6:41. So together animals, shepherds, and children form the ranks of "little ones" to whom Jesus gives the greatest attention. These little ones in turn will give individual attention to others.

Luke's Gospel closes with a story that directly contrasts the "no room at the inn" experience of the traveling strangers, Joseph, Mary, and the child at Bethlehem. Two disciples on Easter Sunday were walking to Emmaus when a stranger met them and began to explain Jesus' death in terms of the Scriptures. On reaching Emmaus, the stranger acted as if he were going on. However the disciples "strongly urged him" to stay with them in their lodging. "So he went in and stayed with them" (24:29). As a result, at supper time, the disciples' eyes were opened and they recognized Jesus in the breaking of the bread (24:30-31). Thus the individual attention and concern for each human person is the direct opposite of the Roman concern for power over the masses in world enrollment. Yet the individual gospel focus will reach the whole world. Jesus closes the gospel with the announcement that "repentance and forgiveness of sins is to be proclaimed in his name to *all peoples of the world"* (24:47).

THE CHILD, LORD AND SAVIOR WITH GOD'S HEAVENLY ARMIES IN CONTRAST TO ROMAN LEGIONS

During the night, a great light indicating the divine presence shone around the shepherds to announce the birth of Jesus: "The Glory of the LORD shone around them" (2:9). This contrasts with the dim glow (if any!) of the "divine halo" around Caesar's head on Roman coins. The angel announced to the shepherds, "I bring you good news of great joy for all the people: to you is born today in the city of David a Savior, who is the Messiah, the Lord." The title "Messiah" *(Christos)* announced the fulfillment of Israel's expectations, but meant little to Romans—except as a possible threat.

However, those of "Lord," *Kyrios,* and "Savior," *Sōtēr* were a different matter. Caesar posed as a savior and protector of the world. *Kyrios,* especially in the eastern more Hellenistic empire, was a title given to the gods of the universe and assumed by many Roman emperors. In contrast, the divine child bears this title, which in the previous verse is attributed to God, as the glory of the LORD shines on the shepherds. In Luke's Gospel, more than any other, Jesus is named as LORD. The Acts of the Apostles begins with Pentecost and Peter's proclamation of prophecy fulfillment: "Everyone who calls on the name of the LORD shall be saved" (2:21). This becomes a theme in all of Acts where the title "Lord" appears over a hundred times.

Immediately afterward, to illustrate the power of these names, "Suddenly there was with the angel a multitude of the heavenly host." The word "host" is a rather weak way to translate a military term, *stratia,* an army. *In God's inner workings, all of Caesar's power and armies are no match for God's power and his heavenly militia.*

THE CONTRAST OF JESUS' INNER PEACE ON EARTH

Before Jesus began his public ministry, the devil tempted him to exercise external power: "Then the devil led him up and showed him in an instant all the kingdoms of the world" (4:4). The "world" is the same word, *oikoumenē*, found in the story of Jesus' birth where Caesar had decreed that the *whole world* should be registered for purposes of taxation, military, and economic control. Jesus rejects the devil's temptation as the exact opposite of worship of God. He answers, "Worship the Lord your God and serve him only." Service and worship of God, with its message of interior peace on earth is the direct opposite to earthly power used to force and compel people into compliance. Luke's Gospel will spell this out by showing how true peace on earth can only come through forgiveness, love, and nonviolence accompanied by courageous witness to the truth.

THE CHILD, MESSIAH OF PEACE IN THE SCRIPTURES

The Prince of Peace in Isaiah

The proclamation "Peace on Earth" heralds Jesus' mission as a Messiah of Peace according to the Scriptures. In his introductory remarks, Luke opened his Gospel by stating that he intended to present "an orderly account of the events that have been fulfilled among us" (1:1). He would expect his audience to know these Scriptures as part of Isaiah, the first prophet he mentions by name (3:1). Principal among these are those referring to the birth of a future messianic descendent of David. Isaiah, in God's name declares: "The people who walked in *darkness* have seen a *great light:* those who lived in a land of deep *darkness*— on them *light has shined.* You have multiplied the nation, *you have increased its joy"* (9:2-3). This is because:

A *child* has been born for us, a *son* given to us; authority rests upon his shoulders; and he is named Wonderful Counselor, Mighty God, Everlasting Father, *Prince of Peace.* His authority shall grow continually, and there shall be *endless peace* for the throne of *David* and his kingdom. He will establish and uphold it with justice and righteousness from this time onward and forevermore. The zeal of the LORD *of hosts* will do this (9:6-7).

The words in italics are those echoed in the Christmas story. Luke is explaining the meaning of Jesus' birth in terms of God's plan in the Scriptures. It is in Bethlehem, city of *David,* where the birth takes place. It is in *darkness* as shepherds watch over their flocks by night (2:8). Suddenly the night is illumined as the "glory of the Lord *shone around them"* (2:9). As in Isaiah, an atmosphere of joy pervades the birth of Jesus. The angel proclaims, I am bringing you good news of *great joy* for all the *people.* The cause of this joy for all this is the birth of an unusual son, as Mary's time arrives to give birth to a *son.* Then, "she gave birth to her first born *son"* (2:6-7).

The word *child* or *infant* is repeated six times in this chapter to link Jesus with the wonderful *child* in Isaiah. A sign will be an *infant* lying in a manger (2:12, 16). The shepherds make known to Mary and Joseph what they had heard about the child. When they brought the *child* to the Temple forty days afterward, the prophet Simeon received him into his arms (2:27). On their return to Nazareth, Luke notes, "The *child* grew and became strong, filled with wisdom; and the favor of God was upon him" (2:40). Later, when the family visited Jerusalem when he was twelve years old, they were unaware that the *child* Jesus stayed in the Temple (2:43).

The angels' message is the promise of "Peace on Earth." The means to accomplish this is no earthly power, but God's own invisible army or host: "Suddenly there appeared with the angel a multitude of the heavenly *host."*

DAVID, THE CHILD KING AND THE CHILD JESUS

Like Jesus, his ancestor David is secretly designated and anointed to be king as a child. God said to Samuel the prophet, "Go fill your horn with oil and set out; I will send you to Jesse the Bethlehemite, for I have promised for myself a king among his sons" (1 Sam 16:1). When Samuel arrived in Bethlehem, the elders of the city were "trembling," fearing that King Saul would hear about an anointing and regard it as a threat to his own kingship. So they asked Samuel if his coming was (literally) in peace. Samuel replied, "[In] peace." Jesse, the father of David, prepared a great welcoming banquet for Samuel. The seven oldest sons of Jesse were present at that dinner. Looking upon the appearance and strength of the oldest son Eliab, Samuel thought, "Surely the Lord's anointed [literally, the *Messiah* of the Lord, in the Greek text, the *Christos*] is now before the LORD" (16:6). But God's voice came to him from within saying that Samuel should not look to appearances, because "The LORD looks on the heart."

The same happened as Samuel went down the line to the other six sons, and he said to Jesse, "The LORD has not chosen any of these." Then Samuel hesitated and asked Jesse, "Are all your sons here?" Jesse replied, "There remains yet the youngest, but he is keeping sheep." The Greek text of the Old Testament used by Luke, translates "youngest" as *mikros*, "the little one." The work of tending sheep was often delegated to children and David was truly "the least," not even invited to this great occasion. Then Samuel said to Jesse, "Send and bring him; for we will not sit down till he comes here." During the meal, God said to Samuel, "Rise and anoint him, for this is the one." "Then Samuel took the horn of oil and anointed him in the presence of his brothers; and the spirit of the LORD came mightily upon David from that day forward" (16:13).

Through comparisons to Luke's story, we can see how the evangelist used the story of David as a means to bring out the meaning of Jesus' birth. Luke mentions *David* five times (to Mary, 1:27, 32; by Zechariah, 1:69; at Jesus' birth, 2:4, 11). *Bethlehem* is named twice (2:4, 15). Like the coming of Samuel for the anointing, the purpose of the child Jesus is *Peace on Earth* not the deposition of King Herod or Caesar. Samuel does not find David at a regal banquet, but in a rustic setting as a child among *shepherds*, other little ones. The shepherds are mentioned in 2:8, 15, 18. Jesse told Samuel that his youngest one was out *keeping the sheep.* This occupation is again recalled in 1 Samuel 16:19; 17:15, 28, 34. The angel at Jesus' birth announces to the shepherds that the child is the *Messiah (Christ) the Lord.* In similar fashion, Samuel came to Jesse's house to find the anointed *(Messiah* or *Christ)* of the Lord (16:6).

THE VICTORY OF THE CHILD/YOUTH OVER
THE GIANT GOLIATH AND THE FORCES OF EVIL

The story of David and Goliath has become a great archetype in history. It illustrates how "little ones" through the help of God can win a decisive victory over even the mightiest powers of evil. Luke knew that story and some of the details make it likely that he used the imagery. The contrast between the child and the giant Goliath is made through striking details. The Philistines were the traditional enemies of Israel. Before the time of David, the Philistines held them in subjugation through superiority in numbers and armor. They had mastered the secret of iron forging and kept the Israelites from making iron weapons by not allowing them to do any kind of iron work (1 Sam 13:19-22). During a revolt, the two armies faced one another on the sides of two mountains separated by a narrow valley (17:1-3). Out of the Philistine camp emerged a giant in heavy armor threatening anyone to individual combat to settle which group would be victorious or slaves to the other. According to the Hebrew text the giant was nine feet tall. But Greek texts, translating from earlier Hebrew texts, trimmed this down to about six feet nine inches, which would be enormous for those times.

In contrast, David was considered too small to be allowed to fight as a soldier. He remained taking care of sheep and going back and forth to the Israelite camp bringing food for his brothers from home in Bethlehem. The giant Goliath taunted the Israelites, saying that he defied the armies of Israel and their God. David heard this and said to those around him, "Who is this uncircumcised Philistine that he should defy the *armies of the living God?*" (17:26). These words are the exact opposite of the giant's boast. It was not a matter of human strength but God's power.

King Saul heard about David's words and sent for him. David said to the king, "Let no one's heart fail because of him [the giant]; your servant will go and fight against the Philistine" (17:33). Saul replied that David could not possibly do so: "You are just a boy [child], and he has been a warrior from his youth." David insisted that his experience as a shepherd in killing even attacking lions and bears gave him confidence. Likewise, "This uncircumcised Philistine shall be like one of them, since he has defied the *armies of the living God.* King Saul then gave him his own bronze helmet, armor, and sword. But the boy could hardly walk with their weight and took them off. He then went to meet Goliath with no military weapons and armor. He only had a simple shepherd's staff, a slingshot, and his trust in God.

The Philistine giant came out with so much armor that he needed an assistant to help carry it. When he saw little David coming to him, he thought the Israelites were trying to taunt him, "for he was only a youth [child], ruddy and handsome in appearance." The Philistine said, "Am I a dog, that you come to me with sticks?" (1 Sam 17:43). Then he cursed David with all the power of the Philistine gods. Then David made his famous reply, "You come to me with sword and spear and javelin; but I come to you in the name of the LORD of hosts, *the God of the armies of Israel* whom you have defiled. This very day I will strike you down and cut off your head" (17:45-46).

I have italicized above the repetition of the *armies of God* to bring out the central point of the story that even a child with the armor of God can overcome the greatest force of earth.

Coming back to Luke and the birth of Jesus, we can better perceive the inner conflict hidden in the story. On one side is Caesar, the Roman Empire and King Herod, its puppet. Luke has placed them there by name (1:5; 2:1). King Herod made Bethlehem one of his prominent military centers. His huge fortress and palace called *Herodium* lay in plain view near Bethlehem. The time of any census was always very dangerous, since they often instigated fierce tax revolts. A large number of Herod's soldiers along with Roman troops of the governor would have been present in Bethlehem to maintain order. On the other side, a seemingly helpless little child is born but God's invisible army, *a multitude of the heavenly host* is more powerful than any earthly force or army. This is the same contrast as in the triple mention of the armies of God and the child facing the enemies of God in the Goliath story.

THE CHRISTMAS CHILD AS MODEL FOR EVERY CHILD

The child in Bethlehem is as fully human as any child at birth. He has not dropped down from heaven as a super-child as some of the later post-biblical apocryphal stories would have people believe. In contrast, the brief account of the birth of Jesus relates that his mother "Gave birth to her firstborn son, wrapped him in *bands of cloth*, and laid him in a manger" (2:7). The older English translations have "swaddling clothes" instead of bands of cloth. The dictionary defines these "swaddling clothes" as "strips of cloth wrapped around a newborn infant to hold its legs and arms still." However, in ancient times the more likely objective was to keep the weak spine of an infant straight. One of the signs for the shepherds was that they would find an infant wrapped in these swaddling clothes (2:12). Since these birth practices were common for every child, it is likely that Luke is emphasizing the utter weakness and humanity of the newborn Messiah.

Luke's intention becomes more likely when we read the only other two references to a child's swaddling clothes in the Scriptures. To describe the utter need of Israel as a child, the prophet Ezekiel describes her as having no one to put swaddling clothes around her (16:7). Also, King Solomon uses the image to bring out his complete humanness at birth:

I also am mortal like everyone else, a descendant of the first-formed child of earth; and in the womb of a mother I was molded into flesh, within the period of ten months, compacted with blood, from the seed of a man and the pleasure of marriage. And when I was born, I began to breathe the common air, and fell upon the kindred earth; my first sound was a cry, as is true of all. I was nursed with care in *swaddling clothes* (Wis 1:1-4).

THE MODEL OF A CHILD GROWING IN WISDOM

Solomon continues his tribute to Wisdom after such humble beginnings: "Therefore I prayed, and understanding was given me; I called on God, and the spirit of wisdom came to me." The same wisdom motif is found in regard to the child Jesus. After his parents had brought him to the Temple, Luke writes, "The *child* grew and became strong, filled with wisdom; and the favor of God was upon him" (2:40). When Jesus was twelve years old he went up to the Temple with his parents for the feast of Passover. Twelve was the age when a child was supposed to take on adult responsibilities. On looking for him before returning home, "they found him in the Temple, sitting among the teachers, listening to them and asking questions" (2:47).

This listening attitude is characteristic of wisdom. As a young man, Solomon had prayed to God for (literally) "a listening heart" so he could make good decisions in regard to his people (1 Kgs 3:9). This attitude continued in Jesus' boyhood: "Then he went down with them and came to Nazareth and was obedient to them [his parents]" (2:51). The verb in Hebrew for "obey" was *shema*, hear. The whole childhood section in Luke ends with the words, "And Jesus increased in wisdom and in years, and in divine and human favor" (2:52).

SUMMARY

The stories of the birth and childhood of Jesus proclaim him to be the hidden promised child-Messiah of peace. This contrasts with the external *Pax Romana* of the Roman emperor which enforced peace and security by overwhelming power to prevent dissension and revolt. The military might of Rome enforced this peace by rigid control. Instead, the child-Messiah has an interior heavenly army of angels at his side to proclaim the good news of Peace on Earth. The scriptural background of the anointing of David, the child shepherd strengthens the strong contrast between powerful earthly rulers and little ones. In addition the child Jesus is a model for every human child in the circumstances of his humble birth. This is confirmed by the wisdom literature.

COROLLARY FOR TODAY

It has been characteristic not only of Rome but of other world empires throughout history until now to promise "peace and security" to fearful people by a "military solution" to dissension, threats to authority, and disagreement. In doing so, they have often appealed to the idea of a holy war against "terrorism and evil-doers" and proclaimed that they were instruments of a God who is fighting on their side for all that is holy and good. Messiahs of peace, in contrast, often find few followers. Their appeal is to children at heart and "little ones" who are like the child of Bethlehem. They are deeply sensitive and responsive to suffering and injustice, as the only real way to achieve "Peace on Earth."

2

Jesus, Messiah of Peace and Nonviolence in the Passion Story

WE MOVE FROM THE BIRTH OF THE CHILD-MESSIAH OF PEACE TO HIS death because the ending of the Gospel reflects its beginning. Thus we will have a firmer basis for Jesus' role as a Messiah of Peace and nonviolence. Luke has planned the passion narrative so his audience will understand their own role as followers of Jesus and peacemakers. We keep in mind that Luke was writing near the end of the first century. Jerusalem had finally succumbed to Rome in A.D. 70 after a long war that ended with the Temple's destruction. However, the violent resistance to Rome still continued in Luke's time and later led to another revolution in A.D. 132–135 under Bar Kochba. This leader was able to restore the Temple sacrifices for a brief period.

JESUS' TRIUMPHANT ENTRY INTO JERUSALEM AND FINAL TEACHINGS ON PEACE

In his final journey to Jerusalem, Jesus approached the Mount of Olives and prepared for a solemn entry into the capital. Luke describes this as a pre-celebration of all which was to happen because of Jesus' message of peace. First there is a detailed instruction about requisitioning a donkey for Jesus' entry. As Jesus rode into the city, his disciples spread out their garments to form a "red carpet" before him. The detailed plans and descriptions point to a scriptural sign. The prophet Zechariah had written:

> Rejoice greatly, O daughter Zion! Shout aloud, O daughter Jerusalem! Lo, your king comes to you; triumphant and victorious is he, humble and riding on a donkey. . . . He will cut off the chariot from Ephraim and the war-horse from Jerusalem . . . and he shall command *peace* to the nations (9:9-10).

The donkey, the joyful shouting, the mention of the king, and the purpose of peace all link together. Jesus does not ride on a triumphant white horse but a humble donkey. His purpose is to do away with military chariots and war horses in order to bring a message of peace. A multitude of disciples praised God, saying, "Blessed is the *king* who comes in the name of the Lord! *Peace* in heaven, and glory in highest heaven" (19:38). Here we notice a parallel to the "peace on earth" birth of Jesus. Luke writes, "Peace in *heaven*" because Jesus will soon be returning there. "Glory in highest heaven" is the same praise as that of the angels at Jesus' birth (2:14). There is a *multitude* of disciples just as there was a multitude of angels at Jesus' birth. However joy soon turns into sorrow as Jesus came near to Jerusalem:

> As he came near and saw the city, he wept over it saying, "If you, even you, had only recognized on this day the things that make for *peace* but they are hidden from your eyes. Indeed, the days will come upon you, when your enemies will set up ramparts around you and will surround you, and hem you in on every side. They will crush you to the ground, you and your children within you, and they will not leave within you one stone upon another; because you did not recognize the time of your visitation from God (19:41-44).

Here Jesus does not describe a generic responsibility of Jerusalem or its people in regard to the war with Rome and the resulting disastrous defeat of its defenders. Josephus's account of this war is one of the most gruesome ever written. However, only a minority of Israel really wanted this war. It was the determined work of violent revolutionaries under military leaders who proclaimed themselves to be prophets or messiahs and invincible instruments of God. The "time of visitation" is Jesus' coming not as a military leader but as a Messiah of peace.

Jesus again describes the fate of Jerusalem and the Temple in his last discourse. When some remarked to Jesus about the beauty of the Temple and its buildings, he predicted a day when "not one stone will be left upon another; all will be thrown down" (21:6). On being asked what signs would point to this, Jesus answered, "Beware that you are not led astray; for many will come in my name and say 'I am he!' and 'the time is near.' Do not go after them" (21:7). These words refer to false leaders proclaiming themselves as messiahs and appealing to people by promising great signs and victories in war like those of Moses in the past. There were many of these in the years before the war with Rome. Even in the second war with Rome from A.D. 132–135, the Jewish leader Bar Kochba declared to the people that he was the Messiah.

Along the same lines, Jesus said, "When you hear of wars and insurrections, do not be terrified; for these things must take place first, but the end will not follow immediately" (21:9). These insurrections would be led by the false messiahs above. However many people believed there would be a final holy war, a great "mother of all wars" against the forces of evil before the end of the world. In this war, God would bring victory despite overwhelming odds. The book of Revelation has references to this type of battle when the "final bowls of God's wrath" were poured out. Demonic spirits, working great signs, assemble all the kings of the earth "for battle on the great day of God almighty" (16:14). They assemble all their forces together "in the place that in Hebrew is called Harmagedon" (16:16) to make war against God's people. Jesus warns against the great deception of many human leaders who try to convince people they are God's chosen leaders leading them to triumphant victory over evil-doers and God's enemies.

THE DECISION FOR NONVIOLENCE
DURING JESUS' AGONY IN THE GARDEN

After his Last Supper, Jesus went with his disciples to the Mount of Olives to pray and make his final decision whether to return to Jerusalem where his life was in immediate danger. He knew that his mission was to preach the good news of the kingdom in the capital city, yet it was still possible for him to withdraw by night to Galilee where his large following afforded him support and safety. His love for Jerusalem impelled him to go there, yet he well knew the experience of prophets of peace before him. He had previously said to his disciples, "Jerusalem, Jerusalem, the city that kills the prophets and stones those who are sent to it! How often have I desired to gather your children together as a hen gathers her brood under her wings, and you were not willing" (13:34)!

Jesus' temptation in the garden is often called "The agony in the garden." However the Greek word *agonia* found only here in Luke means a "painful struggle" rather than only suffering. The episode in Luke sharply differs from that in Matthew and Mark. In Luke, Jesus' prayer prepares for the ensuing temptation of the disciples to attempt a violent resistance. Accordingly, the episode begins and ends with the same words to these disciples, "Pray that you may not come into the time of trial" (22:40). Then Jesus withdrew from them, knelt down on the ground and prayed, "Father, if you are willing, remove this cup from me; yet, not my will but yours be done." When Jesus finished his prayer. Luke writes that the crowd that had come to arrest Jesus suddenly appeared on the scene, led by Judas. Jesus stood his ground and let Judas approach him for the kiss of betrayal.

At his point the surrounding disciples asked Jesus for permission to make a violent defense. They said, "Lord, shall we strike with the sword?" (23:49). However, they did not wait for Jesus' answer. Instead, "One of them struck the slave of the high priest and cut off his right ear." Then Jesus sharply reprimanded the disciples, "No more of this." And to show how much the violence of his followers displeased him, "He touched his ear and healed him." Jesus' own response was in healing, forgiving, nonviolence. The attacking crowd was reinforced with temple police armed with swords and clubs, ready to arrest a violent revolutionary. In contrast, Jesus tells them, "Have you come out with swords and clubs as if I were a bandit?" The translation, "bandit" is of the Greek word, *lēstēs*, that describes the two "bandits" crucified at the right and left of Jesus in the Gospels of Mark and Matthew. It applied to violent revolutionaries who extorted or robbed money from people in order to support their activities. Jesus had no part in such activities. In contrast, he taught openly each day in the Temple. He declares, "When I was with you day after day in the Temple, you did not lay hands on me."

As a final statement at his arrest, Jesus tells the attacking mob, "This is your hour and the power of darkness" (23:53). Luke's Gospel sees trust in violent power as a sign of temptation from Satan. Jesus had already warned against this temptation in his agony in the garden where he twice asked his disciples to pray that they enter not into temptation. From what follows, this temptation was to use violent power to resist Judas and his band. The whole arrest account in Luke is centered about Jesus' refusal to submit to that temptation. Luke also shows that at every step Jesus freely and voluntarily went ahead. He was not a mere helpless victim of those plotting his death. He would not be a Messiah of peace by surrender or submission but by deliberate choice. This was meant to be a model for his followers.

THE TRIAL BEFORE PILATE
AND AFFIRMATION OF JESUS AS MESSIAH OF PEACE

Luke gives more attention to the charges against Jesus than the other Gospels. Because of the dangers of uprisings, Pilate moved his headquarters to Jerusalem for the seven days of the Passover feast. Luke writes that the puppet ruling assembly came before Pilate and accused Jesus, "We found this man perverting our nation, forbidding us to pay taxes to the emperor, and saying that he himself is the Messiah, a king" (23:2). The first of these three charges is better explained in 23:5, when the prosecutors insist: "He stirs up the people by teaching through all Judea, from Galilee where he began even to this place." The claims were ones that would immediately draw the attention of any Roman governor. Anyone who stirs up people or promotes dissension is an enemy of the *Pax Romana*, which every governor made a priority. The question of taxes was always a primary cause of revolts. Jesus' teaching to "Give to the emperor the things that are the emperor's" (20:25) is taken out of the context that it is subordinated to a total service to God: "(Give) to God the things that are God's."

As for proclaiming himself to be a king, a messiah, Jesus never openly proclaimed himself to be one. When Peter declared that Jesus was the Messiah, Jesus rebuked and silenced him (9:21). In regard to being a king, only the Palm Sunday crowd acclaimed Jesus with this title" (19:38). Pilate then directly questioned Jesus: "Are you the king of the Jews?" Jesus answered, "*You* say so." The "you" is emphatic in Greek to emphasize that the words are Pilate's not Jesus' own. Then Pilate told the chief priests and crowds, "I find no basis for an accusation against this man" (23:4). When Pilate heard that Jesus was from Galilee, he sent him to King Herod, who was also in Jerusalem at this time. Jesus refused to answer Herod's questions. In response, Herod's soldiers mocked Jesus over the whole idea of such a powerless figure being a king compared to himself and his thousands of soldiers. So King Herod sent Jesus back to Pilate to confirm his innocence.

A dramatic presentation of Jesus as a man of peace comes when the crowd asks Jesus to release a prisoner according to the Passover custom. They ask for Barabbas, "A man who had been put in prison for an insurrection that had taken place in the city and for murder." Thus Jesus is the very opposite of such a violent revolutionary figure. Pilate then proclaims Jesus' innocence a third time. However, he finally gives in to the crowds assembled by the puppet government and hands Jesus over to the soldiers for crucifixion. Luke heightens the contrast involved by

repeating that Barabbas the violent, even murderous prisoner
was released at the same time (23:25).

THE WAY OF THE CROSS AND
THE FINAL TITLE OF JESUS AS MESSIAH OF PEACE

On the way to Calvary, a crowd largely of women followed
Jesus "beating their breasts and wailing for him" (23:27). Jesus
turned to them and said,

> Daughters of Jerusalem, do not weep for me but for yourselves
> and for your children. For the days are surely coming when they
> will say, "Blessed are the barren, and the wombs that never bore,
> and the breasts that have never nursed." Then they will begin to
> say to the mountains, "Fall on us" and to the hills, "Cover us."
> For if they do this when the wood is green what will happen
> when it is dry? (23:28-29).

These words recall what Jesus had previously said about the
coming horrible destruction of Jerusalem during the war with
Rome (21:20-24). Jesus deeply understood how women were
the first victims of that and every war as they witnessed the destruction of their own children. The war with Rome was initiated
by a minority group that followed military messiahs rather than
leaders like Jesus, a Messiah of peace.

The end of Jesus' life echoes the opening theme of "Peace on
Earth." Crucified to Jesus' right and left were two other men.
Matthew and Mark call them "robbers." But they were "robbers"
in the sense that they were "freedom fighters" opposed to Roman
military occupation. To support their cause they frequently
robbed or extorted money from the populace. Today we might
call them "terrorists." Luke calls them literally, "workers of evil"
or "evil-doers." For the centurion and the soldiers, this was one
more Roman triumph in their holy war against terrorists and evil-
doers threatening the security and peace of a military *Pax Romana*. The soldiers mocked Jesus, saying, "If you are the King of
the Jews, save yourself" (23:27). Luke notes that "there was also

an inscription over him, 'This is the King of the Jews.'" This inscription and the preceding taunt about being King of the Jews are really a message to the gospel audience that Jesus is truly a king through the folly and ignominy of the cross.

However, one of the two men crucified with Jesus began to see things quite differently from the crowds, the soldiers, and even the other crucified man who were taunting Jesus. He rebuked his companion and said, "Do you not fear, since we are under the same sentence of condemnation? And we indeed have been condemned justly for we are getting what we deserve for our deeds, but this man has done no wrong. Then he said, 'Jesus remember me when you come into your kingdom.' Jesus replied, 'Truly, I tell you, today you will be with me in Paradise'" (23:43).

In his last moments Jesus gave his pardon and forgiveness to a terrorist at his side by choosing him to be the first to enter heaven in his company. These concluding words of Jesus proclaim to a gospel audience of any time that a military *Pax Romana* is a delusion not only for the Roman Empire but for all governments who follow the same path. In contrast, true "Peace on Earth" comes through love and forgiveness not through violence, force, and war.

Two striking divine signs confirm Jesus' words: the sun darkens and the veil of the Temple is torn. These herald the opening of the kingdom Jesus promised and the forgiveness of sins, as the Holy of Holies, the exclusive place of forgiveness is now open to all. "Then Jesus, crying with a loud voice said, 'Father into your hands I commend my spirit.' Having said this he breathed his last." These last words of obedient, confident trust in his Father deeply impressed the Roman centurion. "He praised God and said, 'Certainly this man was innocent [literally, "just"].'" This hardened soldier, a specialist in executing revolutionaries and terrorists, admits he has made a mistake regarding Jesus. He has seen that Jesus dies as a Messiah of peace with words of forgiveness acting as the head of an unearthly divine kingdom. Others join the centurion in this recognition as "all the crowds who had gathered for this spectacle saw what had taken place and returned, beating their breasts" (23:49).

THE MESSIAH OF PEACE IN THE RESURRECTION APPEARANCES AND THE SCRIPTURES AS GOD'S PLAN

It is not enough that Jesus is completely innocent of charges of being a military messiah and that he has willingly offered his life rather than being one more helpless victim. Luke must show that the weakness and disgrace of the cross is God's secret plan to save not through human power but through human weakness. The resurrection account that follows is a necessary completion of the cross. The innocence of Jesus along with the resurrection are two concerns connected with the gospel prelude. There Luke announces that he is writing that readers may know the "truth" (in the sense of "certainty") about the things they have been instructed (1:4). The centurion declared, "*Certainly* this man was innocent" (24:47). The same Greek word for "certainly," *ontōs*, is also found in the statement of the disciples, "The Lord has risen *indeed* [certainly] and has appeared to Simon" (24:34). This Greek word is found in Luke in only these two verses.

When the women came to Jesus' tomb on Easter Sunday, they did not find Jesus' body. However, two men in dazzling clothes appeared to them and announced, "Why do you look for the living among the dead. He is not here but has risen" (24:5). Then the angels recalled Jesus' words to them, "Remember, how he told you while he was still in Galilee, that the Son of Man *must* be handed over to sinners, and be crucified, and on the third day rise again." The word "must" is italicized because it refers to God's plan in the Scriptures which are the source of *certainty*. This "remembering" especially concerns the three times that Jesus had predicted his own death and resurrection. However, on each occasion the disciples did not understand because it was the hidden plan of God about the mystery of the cross (9:22, 48; 18:31-34). After this, Luke notes that the women, "remembered his words, and returning from the tomb, they told all this to the eleven and to all the rest" (24:8-9).

The second emphasis on the Scriptures as God's plan takes place during the journey of two disciples from Jerusalem to Emmaus on that same day. While they were walking, a traveler joins them who is really the risen Jesus in disguise. He asks them what they had been discussing. They replied they were talking about Jesus of Nazareth and were deeply disappointed after his condemnation and crucifixion. The stranger scolded them about their slowness to believe in the prophets. Then, "Beginning with Moses and all the prophets, he interpreted to them the things about himself in all the scriptures" (24:27). The Acts of the Apostles cites many of these Scriptures, but the most notable is found in a similar situation as above, when Philip the evangelist meets and converts an Ethiopian official (8:26-40). This official was returning from Jerusalem in his chariot while reading the following prophecy from Isaiah:

> Like a sheep he was led to the slaughter, and like a lamb silent before its shearer, so he does not open his mouth. In his humiliation justice was denied him. Who can describe his generation? For his life is taken away from the earth (53:7-8).

When one passage like this is quoted, the audience is expected to know other verses in the same context. Isaiah describes a dedicated Servant and faithful Israelite in exile who no longer has the consolation and support of Temple worship. However, he does not lose hope but offers his own life, like a nonviolent lamb as a Temple sacrifice for his own people and others. As a result, God announces through Isaiah, "The righteous one, my servant shall make many righteous, and he shall bear their iniquities" (53:11). Also, "He was wounded for our transgressions, crushed for our iniquities; upon him was the punishment that *made us whole*" (53:5). These last words in Hebrew are literally that he (God) "brought his peace" *shalom* on us. The corresponding Greek translation reads literally that (God laid on him) the discipline or teaching of our peace, *eirēnē*. The evangelist Philip drew near the chariot and offered to explain the Scripture to the Ethiopian. Then, "starting with this scripture, he proclaimed to him the good news about Jesus." Philip showed that this Scripture could be applied to Jesus, who voluntarily gave his life in sacrifice for others as a Messiah of peace.

After the travelers arrived in Emmaus, Jesus revealed himself as the mysterious stranger who interpreted the Scriptures. After Jesus vanished, they said to one another, "Were not our hearts burning within us, while he was talking to us on the road, while he was opening the scriptures to us?" (24:32). The disciples then immediately returned to Jerusalem where they found the eleven and others gathered together. While they were talking, Jesus suddenly stood among them and greeted them with the words, "Peace be with you." This greeting on Jesus' part has special energy behind it as Jesus' final greeting. The words summed up Jesus' own special ministry and personal dedication to peace.

The final greeting of peace paves the way for a third reference to the divine plan in Scripture and the disciples' mission to carry Jesus' ministry of peace to the world.

> Then he opened their minds to understand the scriptures, and said to them, "Thus it is written, that the Christ should suffer and on the third day rise from the dead, and that repentance and forgiveness of sins should be preached in his name to all nations, beginning from Jerusalem. You are witnesses of these things. And behold, I send the promise of my Father upon you; but stay in the city, until you are clothed with power from on high" (24:45-49).

In this final commission, we find the ingredients of a peace-centered commission. Designated agents (in his name) of a Messiah of peace are to bring to the world repentance, *metanoia*, forgiveness of sins, and an active witness, *martyres*, in their own lives. The enabling inner presence will be the Spirit, "the promise of my Father" which will clothe them with Jesus' identity and power.

SUMMARY

The references to Jesus as nonviolent Messiah of peace follow one after another in the Passion account. His humble entry into Jerusalem on a donkey fulfill the prophecies of Zechariah about a coming king who puts aside military solutions to obtain peace. The Palm Sunday crowds salute Jesus as king and shout, "Peace in heaven." Jesus weeps over the city because they do not recognize what will bring them peace. Prophesying the destruction of Jerusalem, Jesus warns them not to follow military self-styled messiahs, but to flee the city. Jesus' agony in the garden centers on the temptation to use power. At his arrest he commands his disciples to stop any violent resistance. At his trial both Pilate and Herod find him innocent of being an instigator or military messiah. The choice of Barabbas as a violent revolutionary is a sharp contrast to Jesus. On the way to Calvary, Jesus sympathizes with the women as the first victims of violent wars. On the cross, Jesus freely pardons the repentant terrorist. The Roman centurion has the final word on recognizing Jesus as a just and innocent Messiah of peace. The resurrection accounts confirm this through the appearances of the risen Jesus and proofs from the divine plan in the Scriptures.

COROLLARY FOR TODAY

The word "Christian" means a follower and imitator of Christ (Messiah). Luke wrote in his introduction that he wanted to give Theophilus the truth or certainty concerning the matters about which he had received instruction. Primary for Luke are two statements in his Gospel: the Roman centurion's words, "Certainly, *ontōs*, this man was innocent." This confirmed that Jesus was not a violent revolutionary Messiah, but a Messiah of Peace. The second, "The Lord has risen indeed *[ontōs]*, and has appeared to Simon." This second statement implies succession and continuity of Jesus' work. Therefore the way of Christian is clear: a priority for the way of peace and nonviolence rather than that of force, power, and military solutions.

3

John the Baptist: The Mission to *"Guide Our Feet in the Way of Peace"*

ZECHARIAH, JOHN THE BAPTIST'S FATHER, FILLED WITH THE HOLY Spirit declared that his son was chosen, "To guide our feet in the way of peace" (1:79). In describing John's role, Luke provides us a valuable outline of the main peace themes in his Gospel. The very first words, after the dedication to Theophilus, read, "In the days of King Herod of Judea, there was a priest named Zechariah, who belonged to the priestly order of Abijah. His wife was a descendent of Aaron, and her name was Elizabeth." The mention of Herod has an ominous tone as a king who would surely oppose any rival. This Herod was Herod the Great who ruled from 37 to 4 B.C. Rome supported him as "King of the Jews" a puppet king of Judea. Herod the Great in turn was the father of Herod Antipas who ruled over Galilee at the time of Jesus' ministry. By this time, Pontius Pilate had become the direct governor of Judea and ruled from A.D. 26 to 36. The mention of Herod the Great at the Gospel's beginning foreshadows his role as the opposing force to the Baptist and his mission of peace.

THE BIRTH OF THE BAPTIST AND
THE PROPHECY OF HIS ROLE AS A GUIDE TO PEACE

"Peace," *shalom* in Hebrew, *eirēnē* in Greek, is a very common word in the Bible, found 323 times all together, but many more times indirectly since it was used in every greeting and farewell. To this day in Israel it is the common greeting whether personal, by letter, or on the telephone. Luke's Gospel contains the word fourteen times, more than all the other Gospels combined. It appears as a leading theme in Jesus' preaching. Luke has Peter describe Jesus' ministry in the Acts of the Apostles when he declares that God sent Jesus to Israel "preaching peace" (10:36).

In itself, *shalom* has a broad range of meaning in the area of wholeness, well being, harmony, completion, and fulfillment. Proceeding from these roots are many branches of meaning such as reconciliation, forgiveness, avoidance of conflict, and healing. The author and source of peace is God who spreads this peace through an interconnected universe. Every greeting is really a prayer for peace, whether God's name is directly there or not. So we will not be surprised to find the pre-eminence of peace in the Baptist's story. This begins with predictions of his coming unusual birth and role. These predictions are confirmed by unusual signs.

PREDICTIONS AND UNUSUAL SIGNS
ABOUT THE BAPTIST'S BIRTH AND ROLE

First, his parents were beyond the usual ages of childbearing and child rearing: "They had no children because Elizabeth was barren and both were getting on in years" (1:7). Second, Zechariah was chosen by lot to offer incense in the Temple building on an altar just facing the veiled entrance to the Holy of Holies. Such a privilege might not even happen in a lifetime to a priest. The fact that he was *chosen by lot* pointed to special divine intervention, according to views of that time. Next, he had a terrifying vision of an angel standing beside the altar of incense. But even more awesome was the announcement that he and his aged wife would have a child and that even his name, John, was designated. The announcement of any coming child, of course, would be a shock. But that their child would initiate a turning point in history like the great Elijah was simply overwhelming:

He will turn many of the people of Israel to the LORD their God.
With the spirit and power of Elijah, he will go before him, to
turn the hearts of parents to their children, and the disobedient
to the wisdom of the righteous, to make ready a people prepared for the LORD (1:16-17).

The above quotation forms the last words of Malachi, the last
written prophet of the Hebrew Bible. God promises that he will
send the prophet Elijah again before the last day of the Lord. His
role will be to "turn the hearts of parents to their children and the
hearts of children to their parents" (4:5-6). This "turning to God"
will be expressed in Luke by the word *metanoia*, meaning "to
change one's mind." Later Luke will relate that "the word of God
came to John son of Zechariah in the wilderness. He went into all
the region around the Jordan, proclaiming a baptism of repentance, *metanoia*, for the forgiveness of sins" (3:2-3). This *metanoia*
is mentioned nine times in his Gospel and five times in the Acts
of the Apostles. Here again, more in Luke than the other Gospels
combined. It becomes an important basis for true peace.

Zechariah was so shaken by the apparition and these words
that he could not believe them. He said to the angel, "How will
I know this is so? For I am an old man and my wife is getting on
in years" (1:19). The angel Gabriel replied that Zechariah would
be "mute, unable to speak, until the day that these things occur."
Meanwhile, all the people outside were waiting for him to
emerge from the Temple and wondered at the delay. They were
waiting for the customary blessing of the priest. This blessing
was a transfer of the divine energies in response to the incense
offering of themselves and their prayer. When Zechariah came
out with only nonverbal gestures, they knew he would not be
able to pronounce the climactic priestly blessing. The words for
this blessing were given directly by God to Moses:

> Thus shall you bless the Israelites: You shall say to them,
> The LORD bless you and keep you;
> The LORD make his face to shine upon you, and be gracious to you;
> The LORD lift up his countenance upon you, and give you peace.

So they [the priests] shall put my name on the Israelites, and I will bless them (Num 6:22-27).

We note above the triple name LORD, behind which was the great revelation name YHWH given to Moses at the burning bush near Sinai (Exod 3:14-15). All the people would bow each time that sacred name was mentioned in order to receive God's presence, power, and peace upon them. Luke opens his Gospel with the shocking failure to receive the anticipated blessing of peace because of the lack of Zechariah's faith. We will later see that Luke closes his Gospel with Jesus ascending into heaven and giving his disciples and gospel audience the full priestly blessing of peace.

ELIZABETH TAKES THE INITIATIVE OF FAITH

This woman is the first to believe, like the first women to believe in Jesus' resurrection at the empty tomb (24:8). Luke knows that in this world there can never be *shalom* in the sense of fullness without the equal presence and witness of women. Thus Luke's Gospel is often called the "Gospel of Women." After Elizabeth gave birth, family and friends gathered eight days later for his circumcision and naming. This largely male enclave wanted to name the boy after his father. However, Elizabeth alone took a strong stand in opposition and said, "No; he is to be called John" (1:60). However, the relatives firmly objected, "None of your relatives have this name." Then they made hand signs to Zechariah to get his support. He then signaled for a tablet and wrote, "His name is John." Everyone was amazed at his answer. For Zechariah it was a leap of faith, trusting in his vision and the angel's message. Suddenly he was able to talk again and began to praise God.

Luke writes that "Zechariah was filled with the Holy Spirit and spoke this prophecy." Within this prophecy, Zechariah announced more about the future role of his son, the Baptist:

> You, child, will be called the prophet of the Most High; for you will go before the Lord to prepare his ways, to give knowledge of salvation to his people by the forgiveness of their sins. By the ten-

der mercy of our God, the dawn from on high will break upon
us, to give light to those who sit in darkness and in the shadow
of death, *to guide our feet into the way of peace* (1:76-79).

Here Zechariah tells us where this "guide into the way of
peace" will proceed from. It is translated as "the tender mercy of
our God." Some translations have "compassion of our God" instead. In Greek, it is the *splangchna* of the mercy of God. This
splangchna is literally the "viscera" or "gut feelings" of God that
proceed from his deepest quality of *rachum* in Hebrew, "womb
compassion" from the root *rechem*, meaning "womb." We will
describe this more in detail in chapter 6, the Sermon on the
Plain. There Jesus declares the basis of his teaching: "Be merciful, as your Father is merciful" (6:36). In the words of Zechariah,
this loving compassion arises from God just like the morning
sunrise with its warmth and light.

JOHN THE BAPTIST AT THE JORDAN AS
A GUIDE TO THE WAY OF PEACE

Luke again contrasts the Baptist with the powerful authority
structures at the time when he began his ministry:

> In the fifteenth year of the reign of Emperor Tiberius, when
> Pontius Pilate was governor of Judea, and Herod was ruler of
> Galilee, and his brother Philip ruler of the region of Ituraea and
> Trachonitis, and Lysanias ruler of Abilene, during the high
> priesthood of Annas and Caiaphas, the word of God came to
> John son of Zechariah in the wilderness (3:1-2).

This Herod is the son of Herod the Great at the time of the
birth of Jesus. He is now the ruler of Galilee, while Pontius Pilate
(A.D. 26–36) has taken over direct Roman government of Judea.
Annas, and then Caiaphas were the chief priests and Israel leaders under Rome. They received their appointments from Rome
each year. Both Herod and Pilate were most anxious to maintain
the external *Pax Romana*. While John the Baptist advocated

inner peace and change, the Roman authorities were very wary of any popular movement attracting large crowds of people and stimulating hopes for national Jewish restoration.

The mention of Herod begins and closes the account of the Baptist's ministry. Luke summarizes by writing that John proclaimed good news to the people. "But Herod the ruler, who had been rebuked by him because of Herodias, his brother's wife, and because of all the evil things that Herod had done, added to them all by shutting up John in prison" (3:19-20). This imprisonment was a prelude to his execution, the story of which is related in Mark 6:14-29 and Matthew 14:1-12. John was thus a true prophet, willing to rebuke even the king although this meant danger to his own life. Later we will see how Jesus follows the same path and challenges his followers to do the same. While Jesus is a Messiah of Peace, he does not hesitate to take strong stands against evil even at the risk of his life.

THE BAPTIST'S CALL TO REPENTANCE, *METANOIA*

"The word of God came to John, son of Zechariah, in the wilderness" (3:3). The expression "The word of God came" is the very same description of God's speaking through Jeremiah (1:4) and other prophets in the Bible. The Baptist continues the line of great prophets through the centuries as mouthpieces of God's message. "He (John) went into all the region around the Jordan, proclaiming a baptism of repentance, *metanoia*, for the forgiveness of sins" (3:3).

John's baptism and preaching caused great excitement as the news spread everywhere that a new prophetic voice had arisen. Usually such a baptism was required only of Gentile converts to Judaism. For them it meant the beginning of an entirely new life and covenant with God, as if they were newborn children. In this new life, everything previous had to be carefully sifted. This applied to their marriages, relationships, friendships, associates, and even their professions or work. Only then could they be admitted to God's covenant with the symbolic ceremony of circumcision.

However, John preached that even for Jews, their circumcision was not to be considered as an automatic guarantee of God's favor. John declared that in view of the "wrath to come" (3:7) a whole new beginning and conversion was required. This "wrath to come" was a way to describe a coming great judgment of God. John's stentorian voice warned the crowds who came to him: "You brood of vipers! Who warned you to flee from the wrath to come? Bear fruits worthy of repentance. Do not begin to say to yourselves, 'We have Abraham as our ancestor'; for I tell you, God is able from these stones to raise up children to Abraham" (3:7-8). This meant that serious decisions had to be made about every phase of life and activity: "Even now the ax is lying at the root of the trees; every tree therefore that does not bear good fruit is cut down and thrown into the fire" (3:9).

In making such demands, it is likely that John was influenced by the practices of the Qumran ascetic community living in regions near the Jordan river. Candidates entered that community with a baptism in water and renewed this frequently. They vowed complete obedience to the Torah, with an additional oath to share their possessions. John's baptism, however, was once and for all in view of the coming kingdom and did not entail sharing of possessions, unless it was a matter of justice. In his early years, the Baptist "was in the wilderness [desert] until the day he appeared publicly to Israel" (1:80). There he could have learned about the Qumran way of life or even have been associated with them.

John's holy life was an attracting magnet for the crowds that was a guide to others in the way of peace. The angel Gabriel had told his father that John "must never drink wine or strong drink; even before his birth he will be filled with the Holy Spirit" (1:15). Abstention from alcohol was one of the requirements for Nazarite vows (Num 6:1-21), which were temporary unlike that of the Baptist. In addition, Nazarites were not to cut their hair or shave during this time. In art, John the Baptist is often pictured as a Nazarite with long flowing hair as a sign of dedication to God.

Luke's Gospel has scattered references to John's holy and ascetic life. His example provides an introduction to Jesus' teaching of the Lord's prayer: "As he [Jesus] was praying in a certain place, and after he had finished, one of his disciples said to him, 'Lord, teach us to pray, as John taught his disciples'" (11:1). The reference to the Baptist is apropos for he combined his ministry of preaching with prayers and taught others to do likewise as they lived a common life and helped John in his baptismal ministry.

On another occasion, Luke describes an objection some opponents raised about Jesus' disciples: "John's disciples, like the disciples of the Pharisees, frequently fast and pray, but your disciples eat and drink" (5:33). In a story about a tax collector and a Pharisee, Jesus describes the Pharisee who stood up to pray to God with the words, "I fast twice a week" (18:12). Fasting often accompanied periods of intense prayer because it absorbed all the body energies and focused them on God. All of the above descriptions point to an austere image of the Baptist and a strict ascetic life. Some people regarded him as an extremist: Jesus said, "John has come eating no bread and drinking no wine, and you say, 'He has a demon'; the Son of Man has come eating and drinking and you say, 'Look, a glutton and a drunkard, a friend of tax collectors and sinners'" (7:33-34). However Jesus gave the Baptist a great tribute when he told his disciples,

> What then did you go out to see? A prophet? Yes, I tell you, and more than a prophet. This is the one about whom it is written, "I am sending my messenger ahead of you, who will prepare your way before you." I tell you, among those born of women no one is greater than John; yet the least in the kingdom of God is greater than he (7:26-28).

In this text, Jesus names the Baptist not only a prophet, but the greatest of the prophets—the one destined for his role by God's plan in the Scriptures.

THE REQUIREMENTS OF *METANOIA*

In general, the requirements were the practice of justice and mercy. Since his call was like that of Isaiah, whom Luke names (3:4), the response would imitate that in Isaiah, the great prophet of justice. In our next chapter, we will see how Luke merits the title of being a "gospel of justice." Luke provides particular examples among the crowds that heard John's preaching as an invitation to baptism:

> And the crowds asked him, *"What then should we do?"* In reply he said to them, "Whoever has two coats must share with anyone who has none; and whoever has food must do likewise." Even tax collectors came to be baptized, and they asked him, "Teacher, *what should we do?"* He said to them, "Collect no more than the amount prescribed for you." Soldiers also asked him, "And we, *what should we do?"* He said to them, "Do not extort money from anyone by threats or false accusation, and be satisfied with your wages" (3:10-15).

We have italicized the triple repetition of "what should we do?" This highlights the practical decisions that are essential to *metanoia*. The first is broad and general summarizing the generous sharing of the basics of life in food and clothing. This serves as an introduction to Luke's total gospel focus on justice that we will study in our next chapter. Then we find an answer to people considered the most "hopeless" groups for conversion. These were men who cooperated with the Roman government in regard to tax collection. They are not asked to abandon their scribal profession but to cheat no one, instead of heaping up money by overcharging people. Likewise soldiers are not asked to throw down their weapons but to relinquish violence by not using their power to extort money or other advantages.

This emphasis on "what shall we do" in response to preaching and connected to *metanoia* also appears in Luke's Acts of the Apostles. After Peter addresses the crowds on the first Pentecost day, they were deeply moved and asked, "What shall we do?"

(2:38). Peter answered, "Repent *[metanoēsate]* and be baptized every one of you in the name of Jesus Christ so that your sins may be forgiven; and you will receive the gift of the Holy Spirit." Some of the practical consequences of this directly parallel the first response to the Baptist in regard to food and clothing: "All who believed were together and had all things in common; they would sell their possessions and goods and distribute them to all, as any had need" (Acts 2:44-45).

SUMMARY

The theme of peace begins and ends Luke's Gospel, where it is more prominent than all the other gospels. Zechariah announces the Baptist's role "to guide our feet in the way of peace." This begins like a sunrise with the warm *splangchna* of God's inner compassion. It includes *metanoia*, forgiveness of sin, and the infusion of the Holy Spirit. John's preaching of this inner peace contrasts the forcible outer *Pax Romana* of Herod and Pilate. Yet the Baptist risks and finally loses his life because he is a prophet who fearlessly points out the evil practices of Herod and his kingdom. John's preaching and its practical emphasis on "what shall we do" heralds the preaching of Jesus and introduces Luke's Gospel as a gospel of justice.

COROLLARY FOR TODAY

The practical "what shall we do" emphasis in John's Baptism contrasts the tendency to be a mere bystander or constant critic of all the evil in the world. In our times, Robert McAfee Brown was a modern champion of justice and human rights. Yet he always told his children and others that we should not criticize all the evil we read about in the newspapers, television, and media if we are going to do nothing about it. John the Baptist and Jesus were not mere bystanders as others plunged into waters of baptism and responded with practical action. They entered the waters of the Jordan along with them. It is interesting to read in the story of Philip's conversion of an Ethiopian official that *"both of them,"* Philip and the eunuch went down into the water together (Acts 8:38). In later centuries, the observance of Lent began with the custom of Christians to accompany catechumens in their journey of preparation to enter the waters of baptism.

4

"Justice and Peace Shall Kiss One Another"

Luke's Gospel of Justice

THE ABOVE TEXT IS FROM PSALM 85:11. MOREOVER, IT IS PART OF two verses that describe the inner qualities of God as meeting together and filling the whole earth: "Steadfast love and faithfulness will meet; righteousness (justice) and peace will kiss each other. Faithfulness will spring up from the ground, and righteousness will look down from the sky."

Peace means wholeness and thus it cannot exist where justice is lacking and justice by its very nature produces peace. Thus Isaiah will declare, "The effect of justice will be peace, and the result of righteousness, quietness and trust forever" (32:17). Consequently, justice will be at the very heart of Luke's Gospel. Thus we must study justice in Luke before going on to other chapters. This justice will be based on the biblical view of justice found in the Torah and prophets. That biblical view is rooted in the meaning of the land and God's covenant with his people. Luke begins his story of the Baptist by quoting the prophet Isaiah to point out that John the Baptist is also a prophet and carrier of the same Word of God.

JUSTICE IN THE TORAH AND PROPHETS

The book of Deuteronomy is the preeminent book of the Torah in the Old Testament. Its central issue is God's precious gift of the land and the people's covenant response to God's gift. However, the book is in a time warp with present, past, and future coming together in a way that is often confusing. Theoretically, the people are listening to Moses by the Jordan, yet some provisions in the book hint at previous long-time occupation. For example, the care to respect "boundary markers set up by former generations" (19:14). Also, there is a final covenant curse warning against moving a neighbor's landmark (27:17). The book of Numbers fills in this gap by showing how God divided the land.

A helpful understanding of the ancient land tradition is found in the story of King Ahab's attempt to take away the vineyard of Naboth (1 Kgs 21:1-16). The king cast an envious eye on this adjoining vineyard and wanted to buy it or exchange it for another. But Naboth refused to sell or exchange it, declaring with an oath, "The LORD forbid that I should give you my ancestral inheritance." This refusal is emphasized in the story by a three-fold repetition. The king kept repeating these words to himself, for he knew that he had no power in such a matter. Not even a king could change the ancient laws on hereditary land. Ahab even lost sleep over it and refused to eat.

Queen Jezebel noticed this and took matters into her own hands. She arranged a false accusation to the court that Naboth had cursed God and the king. As a result the court condemned Naboth to death and the king seized the vineyard. At this point God intervened through the prophet Elijah saying, "Go down to meet King Ahab of Israel who rules in Samaria; he is now in the vineyard of Naboth where he has gone to take possession." Because of this serious crime, Elijah tells him that his dynasty will crumble.

From this story we can grasp the importance of each particular ancestral land. It is a designated sacred gift from God that cannot be alienated (except often through sinful intrigue). The enormity of the crime is so great that the great prophet Elijah intervenes with a message from God that this injustice will cause the fall of the king's dynasty. This tradition about the land is either told or reconstructed by the book of Numbers. God instructed Moses and Eleazar the priest to make a census of all of the new generation of Israel that was to enter the promised land (26:1-4). He said:

> To these, the land shall be apportioned for inheritance according to the number of names. To a large tribe you shall give a large inheritance, and to a small tribe you shall give a small inheritance; every tribe shall be given its inheritance according to its enrollment. But the land shall be apportioned by lot; according to the names of the ancestral tribes they shall inherit. Their inheritance shall be apportioned according to lot between the larger and the smaller (Num 26:52-56).

God carefully delineated the boundaries of Israel in Numbers 34. Moses then told the people, "This is the land that you shall inherit by lot" (34:13). Then the representatives of each tribe and the heads of the families further divided the land by lot, finally concluding with the statement: "These are the inheritances that the priest Eleazar and Joshua son of Nun and the heads of the families of the tribes of the Israelites distributed by lot at Shiloh before the LORD, at the entrance of the tent of meeting. So they finished distributing the land" (Jos 19:51).

The equal distribution of the land was supremely important for agricultural economies. Their very existence depended upon it. Professional trades people did exist, yet the average farmer tried to be a jack of all trades to save unnecessary expenses. Any threat to the land was a threat to life. So if they saw that one family had overabundance and they did not have enough, this was evil in itself.

Putting together the views on the land in Deuteronomy and Numbers we have the following: Biblical justice is built on three pillars: (1) scarcity of the land—this particular geographic area; (2) the land is an inherited designated gift of God that should never be alienated; (3) it is a land "equally" (land can never be perfectly shared) divided by divine lot to tribes and then to families. In regard to no. 2 the geographical area is not theirs through conquest but through a promise made to Abraham and repeated often to Isaac, Jacob (Israel) and their descendants. Justice in the prophets will be based on this view of the land in the Torah. Some examples will follow.

THE WAY OF JUSTICE IN ISAIAH

Isaiah begins with God's absolute challenge: "Hear, O heavens, and listen, O earth; for the LORD has spoken: I reared children and brought them up, but they have rebelled against me. The ox knows its owner, and the donkey its master's crib; but Israel does not know, my people do not understand" (1:1-2). In this scathing introduction, God declares that seemingly dumb animals like an ox and donkey know where to go for their food and nourishment, but his people do not know. All through Isaiah, a central theme will be to *know the Lord* in a deep sense. This will involve every facet of life, but will be summed up in justice. Later, in preparing a way for the Lord's return it will be called a "way of justice" (40:14), a description later taken over by Matthew to describe the way of John the Baptist and Jesus (21:32; 3:15). Justice is so close to God's nature that he will declare, "I the LORD love justice" (Isa 61:8).

Isaiah's presentation consists of various stages, although not in strict logical order:

1. Judgment time is near—*that day* or *day of God* occurs nine times in chapters 1-5. God's intervention as a judge is coming soon because evil has reached a climax.

2. A description of evil works and the sorry condition of the people, e.g.,

> Ah, sinful nation, people laden with iniquity, offspring who do evil, children who deal corruptly, who have forsaken the LORD, who have despised the Holy One of Israel, who are utterly estranged! Why do you seek further beatings? Why do you continue to rebel? The whole head is sick, and the whole heart faint. From the sole of the foot even to the head, there is no soundness in it, but bruises and sores and bleeding wounds (1:4-6).

In a city that was once faithful and "full of justice," now "they do not defend the orphan and the widow's cause does not come before them" (1:23). In regard to the land, the rich gobble up the lands of the poor: "Ah, you who join house to house, who add field to field, until there is room for no one but you, and you are left to live alone in the midst of the land" (5:8-9).

3. Invitation to change and assurance of forgiveness:

> Wash yourselves; make yourselves clean; remove the evil of your doings from before my eyes . . . come now, . . . says the LORD: though your sins are like scarlet, they shall be like snow; though they are red like crimson, they shall become like wool (1:16-18).

4. Justice as a sign of repentance:

> Cease to do evil, learn to do good; seek justice, rescue the oppressed, defend the orphan, plead for the widow (1:16-17).

5. Hope for the future:

If there is true repentance, Jerusalem will once more be a "city of justice" (1:26). And some day it will be a center where the world's nations will come to learn justice, avoid war, and establish peace. As a result, "nation shall not lift up the sword against nation, neither shall they learn war any more" (2:1-4).

So far, what we have heard is God's plea for a return to the core of the Sinai covenant, if we take the central issues of the land and those deprived of land such as the widows, oppressed and orphans.

TRUE LITURGY: WORSHIP AND OPENNESS TO THE POOR AND OPPRESSED

In the third part of Isaiah, the returned exiles came back joyfully to rebuild the Temple and enjoy the beautiful liturgies and worship. However some became so wrapped up in their devotions that they did not turn outwardly to those in need. God speaks through Isaiah to warn them:

Is not this the fast that I choose: to loose the bonds of injustice, to undo the thongs of the yoke, to let the oppressed go free, and to break every yoke? Is it not to share your bread with the hungry, and bring the homeless poor into your house; when you see the naked, to cover them, and not to hide yourself from your own kin? Then your light shall break forth like the dawn (58:6-8).

God will answer prayers only when liturgy is accompanied by this outreach in justice to others: "Then you shall call, and the LORD will answer; you shall cry for help, and he will say, 'Here I am'" (58:9).

AMOS, SHEPHERD AND PROPHET

The first words of this book inform us that Amos was a shepherd from a little town of Tekoa in Judea about ten miles south of Jerusalem. His prophetic activity, however, took place in the northern kingdom of Israel. He describes his call as follows: "I am no prophet, nor a prophet's son; but I am a herdsman, and a dresser of sycamore trees, and the LORD took me from following the flock, and the LORD said to me, 'Go, prophesy to my people Israel'" (7:14-15).

As a shepherd, Amos lived most of his life outdoors. The great events of his life were sunrise and sunset. He felt God's presence as he watched the stars at night and welcomed the sun as well as the rain. All shepherds love open spaces and freedom. He implores the people to "seek the Lord and live." He is "the one who made the Pleiades and Orion, and turns deep darkness into the morning, and darkens the day into night, and calls for the waters of the sea, and pours them out on the surface of the earth" (5:8).

This awareness of the beautiful harmony of God's creation intensified his shock as he came near wealthy cities like Samaria and Bethel. The sight of so much injustice made him certain that God could not endure this much longer and that a day of the Lord, a day of reckoning was at hand: "Thus says the LORD": For three transgressions of Israel, and for four, I will not revoke the punishment; because they sell the righteous for silver, and the needy for a pair of sandals—they who trample the head of the poor into the dust of the earth, and push the afflicted out of the way; father and son go in to the same girl, so that my holy name is profaned (2:6-7).

"Selling the righteous for silver" means debt slavery for failure to meet obligations. The trampling of the poor and afflicted refers to unjust decisions of judges and elders at the "gates" of the city where such judgments take place. With a shepherd's special sensitivity about the land he announces God's judgment on those who accumulate extra homes and property while others have insufficient to live on: "I will tear down the winter house as well as the summer house; and the houses of ivory shall perish, and the great houses shall come to an end, says the LORD" (3:15). Amos is especially concerned about the contrast between religion and justice. People often came to religious shrines trusting that God would hear their prayers despite injustice to the poor. God says:

> I hate, I despise your festivals, and I take no delight in your solemn assemblies. Even though you offer me your burnt offerings and grain offerings, I will not accept them; and the offerings of well-being of your fatted animals I will not look upon. Take away from me the noise of your songs; I will not listen to the melody of your harps. But let justice roll down like waters, and righteousness like an ever-flowing stream (5:21-24).

These poetic texts contrast the noisy music of religious songs with the pleasing melody of justice that is constant and flowing like a stream. The Hebrew text brings this music out with plays on sounds and words.

JEREMIAH: THE TEMPLE SERMON AND RETURN TO THE CORE OF THE COVENANT

Jeremiah had to publicly confront the views of leaders and false prophets with the basic teachings of the covenant. The Lord told him to stand at the gate of the Temple area and tell the people who entered these words:

Do not trust in these deceptive words: "This is the temple of the LORD, the temple of the LORD, the temple of the LORD." For if you truly amend your ways and your doings, if you truly act justly one with another, if you do not oppress the alien, the orphan, and the widow, or shed innocent blood in this place, and if you do not go after other gods to your own hurt, then I will dwell with you in this place, in the land that I gave of old to your ancestors forever and ever (7:4-7).

The false prophets had continually repeated "This is the temple of the LORD" as a sign of God's unconditional protection for his people. In contrast, Jeremiah repeats the basic core of the covenant around which the Temple was built. This meant elimination of oppression of the alien, orphan, and widow as well as violent shedding of blood. However, the king and his generals were looking to military solutions in an unholy alliance between religion and power politics. This has always been the greatest obstacle to justice. The king, as we have seen in Deuteronomy and Isaiah, was obliged to direct the work of justice. But if most of the resources of a small country were given over to the military, this could not be done. In addition, there was the great deception that people were encouraged to believe that fighting against "God's enemies" was heroic service of God. Throughout history, unholy alliances between religion and the military have caused terrible sufferings and the loss of resources that could be given to the pursuit of justice.

JUSTICE IN LUKE'S GOSPEL

The views on money and possessions in Luke are based on those we have seen in the Torah and Prophets. Therefore, they are opposed to an attitude that generosity on the part of the affluent is sufficient. This view is based on an imaginary world of unlimited resources, with the consequence that the over abundance of some does not affect others. In contrast, prophetic justice is built on the realistic view of the earth's limited resources which God has designed to be equally shared. *Thus, for some to have less than enough, while others have more than enough is regarded as evil in itself.* This will explain the sharp focus in Luke on money and possessions and the responsibilities connected with them.

As we have seen at the end of chapter 3, John the Baptist asked for complete sharing of food and clothing. These were substantial demands. This goes along with the radical message of the prophets. Tax collectors made much more than their salary through extra charges. Roman soldiers used their power to gain many advantages their minimal allowance could not provide them.

A MODEL CONVERSION FOR LUKE'S AUDIENCE

As an example for the gospel audience, Luke describes the conversion of Zacchaeus, a rich chief tax collector. This occurs at a key juncture just before the end of Jesus' journey to Jerusalem (19:1-10). Zacchaeus was "short in stature" in more ways than one and climbed up a tree to see Jesus as he passed by on the road to Jericho. Jesus must surely have laughed when he saw him up the tree and called, "Zacchaeus, hurry and come down; I must stay at your house today." Zacchaeus was overjoyed by these words and hurried down to welcome Jesus into his home. Many other people, however, were not happy at all. They recalled how often Zacchaeus had defrauded them on their tax bills. Surely the Master could have made a better choice of a house in which to stay and enjoy hospitality. They complained, "He has gone to be the guest of one who is a sinner."

Zacchaeus heard the murmuring and quickly responded. He stood up and said Jesus, "Look, half of my possessions, Lord, I will give to the poor; and if I have defrauded anyone of anything, I will pay them back four times as much." This restitution of fraud was beyond the requirements of biblical law which called for full restitution plus one fifth (Lev 6:1-7). However, the equal sharing of half of his possessions with the poor was an effort to fulfill prophetic justice which was not satisfied with generous gifts, but moved toward equality.

Generous giving out of abundance does not satisfy the requirements of justice. Luke has Jesus make a comparison between rich people who gave from abundance to a poor widow who could only contribute two small copper coins: "Truly this poor widow has put in more than all of them; for all of them have contributed out of their abundance, but she out of her poverty has put in all she had to live on" (21:1-4).

The Acts of the Apostles provides examples of people in the Jerusalem church who voluntarily chose to have much less so others could have a sufficient amount: "All who believed were together and held all things in common; they would sell their possessions and distribute the proceeds to all, as any had need" (2:44-45). It is noteworthy that this comes soon after Peter's first sermon on Pentecost day after the crowds ask him, "What shall we do?" (2:37). Also, "There was not a needy person among them, for as many as owned lands or houses sold them and brought the proceeds of what was sold. They laid it at the apostles' feet, and it was distributed to each as any had need" (4:34-35). Singled out by name is an early believer named Barnabas: "He sold a field that belonged to him, then brought the money and laid it at the apostles' feet" (2:36).

JESUS' INAUGURAL SERMON
AND JUBILEE PLATFORM FOR THE POOR

After his temptation Jesus begins his ministry in Galilee and comes to Nazareth where he was brought up. On the Sabbath day, he goes to the synagogue where he is asked to speak. Luke takes advantage of this occasion to summarize Jesus' mission and teaching. This is Jesus' first sermon and the gospel audience is present in spirit listening with great attention: "The eyes of all the synagogue were fixed upon him" (4:20):

> He stood up to read and the scroll of Isaiah the prophet was given to him. He unrolled the scroll and found the place where it was written, "The Spirit of the LORD is upon me, because he has anointed me to bring good news to the poor. He has sent me to proclaim release to the captives and recovery of sight to the

blind, to let the oppressed go free, to proclaim the year of the
LORD's favor." And he rolled up the scroll, gave it back to the at-
tendant, and sat down. . . . Then he began to say to them,
"Today this scripture has been fulfilled in your hearing" (4:16-
21; Isa 61:1-22).

The word "poor" will be found more often in Luke than any
other Gospel, almost as much as all of them. The poor will receive the first blessing in Luke's beatitudes: "Blessed are you
poor, for yours is the kingdom of heaven" (6:20). This is followed by a woe on the rich (6:23). However, nowhere is the idea
expressed that it is good to be destitute or in serious need. The
word "poor" will have various nuances, but a basic meaning is
that their blessing will come from Jesus' requirements of justice
with the resulting sharing of goods that will come to the poor.

Jesus said the Scripture was fulfilled, because the words described one whom God anointed, *echrisen,* and because he took
upon himself the role described. Originally Isaiah proclaimed the
good news of Israel's freedom from captivity and the return of
the land to homeless, poor exiles returning from captivity. However, Jesus saw that this was not yet realized and made it his mission. The terms used by Isaiah seem influenced by the Jubilee
texts in Leviticus. This was the great *year* of God's favor. The
word for "release," *aphesis,* of the captives is the same word used
to describe the Jubilee: a year of *aphesis* (Lev 25:13).

In the biblical jubilee year, every fiftieth year, all property that
had been alienated from their original owners through debts and
mortgages were to be returned to their original owners. This was
so the principle of just and equal sharing of property could be kept
in a basically agricultural economy. Luke makes the spirit of the
jubilee year a special focus of his Gospel. He will do this through
the priority Jesus gives to the poor. Jesus' first words at Nazareth
(and of the Gospel) are that God has anointed him (as Messiah)
to "bring good news to the poor" (4:18). These words will be repeated again when John the Baptist sends messengers from
prison to ask if he is the chosen one sent by God. Jesus answers

with a concluding sign, "The poor have good news preached to them" (7:22).

JUSTICE FOR THE POOR
AND THE STIFLING EFFECTS OF RICHES

While Jesus brings good news to the poor and pronounces a blessing upon them in a very practical way, he knows that real sharing will not take place until those with superabundance loosen up their purse strings. The following are examples of his teaching.

THE SEED PARABLE

In explaining the seed parable, Jesus declares that the seed is the *Word of God*. This is the same word that came to Isaiah, John the Baptist, Jesus himself, and later ministers of the word. This seed is superabundant and powerful. But Luke focuses on the heart. Jesus says that some seed fell among thorns. "These are those who hear but as they go on their way, they are choked by the cares and riches and pleasures of life, and their fruit does not mature" (8:14). In other words, they produce nothing. In contrast, regarding the seed falling on good soil, "These are the ones who, when they hear the word, hold it fast in an honest and good heart, and bear fruit with patient endurance." This is the miraculous hundred-fold harvest in the parable, that far exceeds any possible human expectation. It is like that of Isaac when he sowed his first crop in the Promised Land and God gave him a miraculous hundred-fold harvest (Gen 26:12).

THE LORD'S POOR AND THE FORGIVENESS OF DEBTS

"And Forgive Us Our Sins, for We Ourselves Forgive Everyone Indebted to Us" (11:4).

This is from Luke's version of the Lord's Prayer. There are signs that this forgiveness includes not only personal offenses but the great financial sin of the heavy burdens of debt laid upon the poor that cause them to lose their land and possessions. This meaning makes the Sermon on the Plain reference to debt more understandable. First, we note the differences with the corresponding petition in Matthew: "And forgive us our debts, as we also have forgiven our debtors" (6:12). In regard to God, Luke has the more generic and understandable "sins," *hamartias* instead of "debts." In reference to other people, Luke is more specific in writing literally "every person owing us." The verb tense is also present instead of the Greek perfect in Matthew. This makes it a more continual process. In Luke's Sermon on the Plain, there is another reference to what amounts to forgiving a debt even in advance with Jesus' saying, "Lend, expecting nothing in return" (6:35). Matthew and Luke provide the same message in this petition, "a perpetual jubilee" to provide relief for the poor laden by debts.

DEBTS IN LUKE'S GOSPEL AND THE LORD'S PRAYER

Like Matthew, Luke has the golden rule as a model for action "Do to others as you would have them do to you" (6:31). As an example of this, Jesus says, "If you lend to those from whom you hope to receive, what credit is that to you? Even sinners lend to sinners, to receive as much again. But love your enemies, do good and lend, expecting nothing in return. Your reward will be great and you will be children of the Most High; for he is kind to the ungrateful and the wicked. Be merciful, just as your Father is merciful" (6:34-35). This double mention of "lending" illustrates its central importance.

A first reaction to the above statement might be a temptation to dismiss it as "impossible ethics." However the instructions surrounding the sabbatical year for debt release in Deuteronomy 15:1-11 are a precedent in the Torah that continued through the centuries, The description of this year starts as follows: "Every seventh year you shall make a release (*aphesis*, the root word in the Lord's Prayer). And this is the manner of the release: every creditor shall remit, *apheses,* what your neighbor owes, *opheilei"* as in the Lord's Prayer (Deut 15:1). However there is a warning near the end: "Be careful that you do not entertain a mean thought, thinking, 'The seventh year, the year of release is near,' and therefore view your needy neighbor with hostility and give nothing; your neighbor might cry to the LORD against you, and you would incur guilt" (15:9). The connection to the Lord's Prayer both in the language of Deuteronomy and in Luke regard lending when there is little hope of return is significant.

A second connection between debts and sin is found only in the story of the Penitent Woman (7:36-50). Simon the Pharisee was shocked by the lavish display of affection that a woman of the city demonstrated by bathing Jesus' feet with her tears and drying them with her hair, along with kissing and anointing them. In response, Jesus gave this illustration: "A certain creditor had two debtors; one owed five hundred denarii, and the other fifty. When they could not pay, he canceled the debts for both of them [the verb is *echarisato,* from the root *charis,* 'favor' or 'grace']. Now which of them will love him more?" The Pharisee replied, "I suppose the one for whom he canceled the greater debt." Jesus concluded by saying, "Therefore I tell you, her sins, which were many, have been forgiven; hence she has shown great love. But the one to whom little is forgiven, loves little." Several points are significant. A debt forgiveness is placed on parallel with a sin forgiveness. Also the same verb, *aphiemi,* release or forgive is used for forgiveness of sin and the forgiveness of a debt. In both cases, they are the result of love. This parallels Luke's Lord's Prayer petition.

THE RICH FOOL AND THE PERILS OF WEALTH

Luke introduces this parable with Jesus' refusal to arbitrate in an inheritance dispute and his warning: "Take care! Be on your guard against all kinds of greed; for one's life does not consist in the abundance of possessions" (12:15). Here a rich man kept storing away more grain and goods to provide for a comfortable retirement in which he could say, "Soul *[psychē],* you have ample goods laid up for many years; relax, eat, drink, be merry." But God said to him, "You fool! This very night your life, *psychē*, is required of you. And the things you have prepared, whose will they be?" Here we see a contrast: a continual search for more possessions has left out God who alone is the master of *life* and death. There is a hint that all the preparations will now be going to others indiscriminately when they could have been freely given to God's poor during lifetime. So the parable concludes, "So it is with those who store up treasures for themselves but are not rich toward God" (12:21).

The above parable is followed by a series of teachings: First, on the priority of the kingdom over life, food, drink, and clothing leading to the axiom, "It is the nations of the world that strive after all these things, and your Father knows that you need them. Instead, strive for his kingdom, and these things will be given to you as well" (12:30-31). Yet this striving is not just pure will-power leading to fears of failure; God's kingdom is a gift to little ones. So Jesus assures his disciples: "Do not be afraid, little flock, for it is your Father's good pleasure to give you the kingdom. Sell your possessions, and give alms. Make purses for yourselves that do not wear out, an unfailing treasure in heaven, where no thief comes near and no moth destroys. For where your treasure is, there your heart will be also" (12:23-34).

THE RICH MAN AND THE POOR MAN
LAZARUS AT THE GATE

Luke wants to show that the coming of the kingdom will bring about a great reversal of values: the poor will find themselves the recipients of God's blessings while the rich will find themselves left empty. Luke is so concerned about this paradox that he spends more time on it than the other three Gospels combined. Perhaps the most dramatic contrast is found in this story:

> There was a rich man who was dressed in purple and fine linen and who feasted sumptuously every day. And at his gate lay a

poor man named Lazarus, covered with sores, who longed to
satisfy his hunger with what fell from the rich man's table; even
the dogs would come and lick his sores (16:19-21).

According to popular mentality, the rich man looked upon
himself as blessed by God. In the same view, most people would
have thought that the poor man had lost God's favor through his
sins, especially laziness. However a dramatic unchangeable reversal takes place after death:

> The poor man died and was carried away by the angels to be
> with Abraham. The rich man also died and was buried. In
> Hades, where he was being tormented, he looked up and saw
> Abraham far away with Lazarus by his side. He called out,
> "Father Abraham, have mercy on me, and send Lazarus to dip
> the tip of his finger in water and cool my tongue; for I am in
> agony in these flames" (16:22-24).

The traditional picture of the afterlife may distract a modern
reader to believe that the story is only about judgment after
death—the furniture of heaven or the temperature of hell. But
Luke has much more than this in mind. The emphasis is on *now*,
a favorite word in Luke. The reversal is in terms of Jesus' present announcement of a kingdom where the poor find themselves
rich and happy while the "rich" become poor and sad (as we see
in the next story).

THE ONE THING LACKING TO A RICH OFFICIAL

A reader has natural sympathy for this official who came to
Jesus asking what he must do to obtain eternal life. Jesus led him
on gradually to an answer by first repeating basic parts of the ten
commandments. The official replied, "I have kept all these since
my youth" (18:21). This was certainly an admirable statement,
yet Jesus responded, "'There is still one thing lacking. Sell all that
you own and distribute the money to the poor, and you will have
treasure in heaven; then come, follow me.' But when he heard
this, he became sad; for he was very rich" (18:22-23).

Jesus' statement has deep implications. He did not come on earth to enforce the ten commandments nor to reveal the heaven and hell in the previous story. These were already part of religious beliefs at that time. The "One thing lacking" is the justice requirements for priority of the poor that are learned by following Jesus in discipleship. So the official "became sad, for he was very rich." He was unable to make that commitment.

The message of the story is so important that Jesus repeats its basic teaching twice. First, he looks directly at the official and says, "How hard it is for those who have wealth to enter the kingdom of God!" Then he adds, even more emphatically, "It is easier for a camel to go through the eye of a needle than for someone who is rich to enter the kingdom of God." This appears so difficult that his disciples exclaimed, "Then who can be saved?" Jesus replied, "What is impossible for mortals is possible with God." In other words, the attraction and seduction of wealth is so great that it easily becomes an addiction that can only be overcome with the help of God through intense prayer.

SUMMARY

In the Bible peace means wholeness and cannot be present without justice. Biblical justice is not the same as generous sharing. In the Torah and Prophets justice is built on the following premises: (1) scarcity of the land and resources, (2) the land is an inherited designated gift of God that should never be alienated, (3) it is a land "equally" (land can never be perfectly shared) divided by divine lot to tribes and then to families, and (4) over abundance of land or possessions when others have less than they need is inherently evil. With this in view, Luke presents the priority of "good news for the poor" in Jesus' first sermon at Nazareth. This is supported by Luke's Sermon on the Plain and illustrated by parables, stories, and Jesus' own example. Riches themselves are presented as a snare and seduction whose power is such that they become an addiction that can only be overcome with God's special help.

COROLLARY FOR TODAY

More and more we are realizing that we are living on a small planet with limited resources. It can no longer be maintained that generous giving on the part of those who have is sufficient to remedy the poverty and suffering of most of the world's population. Globalization has benefited many people, but has helped the rich much more than it has the poor (who have even been sometimes more impoverished). On the grass roots level it is hard to realize that my over abundance when others do not have enough is as evil as Luke's Gospel presents it. But this is due to the fact that many of us are so insulated from that other world of poverty afflicting about 80 percent of the people in this world. We could see, be exposed to, and touched by them if we really wanted to, but the truth is that we have been addicted to holding onto what we have. Addictions are hard to overcome. Jesus in Luke tells us we can succeed by a total dedication to the priority of the poor supported by fervent prayer. Yet the individual is by no means powerless.

In the Lord's Prayer we ask God for forgiveness just as "we ourselves forgive everyone indebted to us." This jubilee spirit has partly influenced the decision of many countries, banks, and organizations to forgive debts of impoverished nations or groups. This movement is a ray of hope for countries in desperate financial straits. However, this does not leave out individual responsibilities. The great world corporations are supported by hosts of individual investors—who are literally money lenders. Much of this money comes from pension funds that pour billions of dollars each month into investments chosen by workers.

In a worldly sense, "a prudent investor" looks for the highest yield with maximum safety regardless of the source from which it comes. In this view investments with largely military oriented focus are the best since the American government alone destines more than a billion dollars a day for the military. Yet it is quite possible today to develop a "peace portfolio" that invests money to be used to build up and not destroy both environment and people. Many pension funds now have the possibility of making the choice of such funds. They are often not as profitable on the short run, but on the long run the best investment is in life itself, peace and justice, not death.

5

The Inner Sources of Peace: Forgiveness and *Metanoia*

LUKE IS PAR EXCELLENCE THE GOSPEL OF *METANOIA*. HE USES THE word or verb fourteen times, more than the other Gospels combined. His Acts of the Apostles mentions it in eleven. In fact, Luke is unique in combining both words, forgiveness and *metanoia*, both at the beginning of the Baptist's ministry and at the end when Jesus commissions his disciples to continue his work. At the beginning "the word of God came to John son of Zechariah in the wilderness. He went into all the region around the Jordan, proclaiming a baptism of repentance, *metanoia* for the forgiveness of sins . . . " (3:2-3). At the end Jesus declares to his disciples that "repentance *[metanoia]* and forgiveness of sins is to be proclaimed in his name to all nations, beginning from Jerusalem" (24:47).

The Greek word has even found a place in the English dictionary where it is defined as a profound, usually spiritual change or conversion. Literally, in Greek, it meant a change of mind. This would conform to Greek views of the priority of the mind. However, the Hebrew world thought in terms of the whole person. Hence it would be a "turning around" to the ways of God and justice and thus away from evil or injustice. The Latin *conversio* would render better the Hebrew mentality.

To better understand forgiveness and *metanoia* together with their close connection to peace, we will follow their occurrence in sequence through the Gospel. We have already studied this in John the Baptist in chapter 3, so we will go immediately to Jesus' ministry.

JESUS' EXTRAORDINARY POWER TO FORGIVE

The Hebrew Scriptures bear witness to God's frequent forgiveness. However, complete and lavish release of sins was something reserved for the final messianic times according to the prophets (e.g., Ezek 36:2; Jer 31:34; Zech 12:10). In Luke's intention to instruct about the things *fulfilled among us* (1:1), he gives more attention to this than any other Gospel. Thus we find that the story of the paralytic's healing and Jesus' power to forgive (5:17-26) receives special attention in Luke. This Gospel has all the authorities and "experts" from a wide region on hand for the event: "One day, while he was teaching, Pharisees and teachers of the law were sitting near by (they had come from every village of Galilee and Judea and from Jerusalem); and the power of the Lord was with him to heal." This power from God included both healing and forgiving.

First, the healing is described in unusual detail: the paralyzed man is let down through the roof because of the crowd and brought before Jesus; the special faith of those who brought him is noted; the verb "forgive" occurs four times. But the focus is on the words of Jesus: "Friend, your sins are forgiven you." The verb is passive, indicating God's action and that Jesus is the agent in proclaiming this. This provokes the challenge of the "experts" who declare, "Who can forgive sins but God only?" (5:21). Jesus confirms his statement by healing the paralytic who immediately stood at Jesus' command, took up his bed, and went home glorifying God.

Jesus' preceding statement and purpose is supremely important for the gospel audience: "But so that you may know that the Son of Man has authority on earth to forgive sins" (5:24). The title "Son of Man" occurs twenty-five times in Luke, sometimes meaning only "human" but mostly referring to a future agent of God. The fact that it is "authority *on earth*" emphasizes that it is something here and now, not the future. The conclusion describes the special awe of human beings at the presence and power of God. Not only the paralytic returned home glorifying God, but "amazement seized all of them, and they glorified God and were filled with awe, saying, 'We have seen strange things *(paradoxa)* today'" (5:26). The word *paradoxa* found only here in the New Testament highlights the special significance of this event. The word *today* is a favorite with Luke, used more by him than the other Gospels combined. It indicates the importance of the present moment in salvation history.

THE LAVISH FORGIVENESS THAT FOLLOWS

> After this he went out and saw a tax collector named Levi, sitting at the tax booth; and he said to him, "Follow me." And he got up, left everything, and followed him (5:27-28).

A tax collector was the notorious enemy of the common people. This was not only because he took their money but because he worked for a foreign occupation force in doing so and often exacted more money than was allotted to him. Jesus' call to Levi was really the forgiveness of an enemy. The brief introduction describes Jesus going out to see Levi. This draws attention to Jesus' initiative in the process of *metanoia*. At the end, Jesus refers to it as a call, "I have come to call . . . " (5:32). "Call" or "name" is another favorite Lukan word occurring forty-two times in his Gospel. This compares with thirty in the other Gospels. It is part of his special theme of *charis* meaning grace, favor, surprise, or gift. *Charis* occurs twenty-five times in this Gospel and Acts as compared with only twice elsewhere in John.

Following this, "Levi gave a great banquet for him in his house; and there was a large crowd of tax collectors and others sitting at the table with them." This immediately drew criticism from the observant religion teachers who asked why they ate with tax collectors and sinners. Eating together with such company was tantamount to close association and an expression of a covenant of peace since they were welcomed to the banquet with the embrace and words of peace. The criticism of Jesus' eating with such people is repeated in the Gospel. Jesus tells others that he is considered "a friend of tax collectors and sinners" (7:34). Later, the Pharisees and the scribes grumbled, "This fellow welcomes sinners and eats with them" (15:2).

In the first two Gospels, the story ends with Jesus saying that he has not come to call the righteous but sinners. However, Luke significantly adds "to repentance" *metanoia* (5:32). Luke wants the audience to be sure to include the whole process of conversion and personal reconciliation of peace when former enemies join and break the bread of covenant with Jesus and his disciples. The next passage about new and old wine is meant to illustrate the characteristic spirit of this *metanoia*.

There were two atmospheres surrounding *metanoia:* the solemn, ascetic manner of the Baptist and the Pharisees and the more joyful one of Jesus and his disciples: "Then they said to him, 'John's disciples, like the disciples of the Pharisees, frequently fast and pray, but your disciples eat and drink'" (5:33). Jesus replied by comparing his own practice to that of a joyful wedding where the guests were hosted with abundant meals and wine for seven days. He told them that his new joyful wine of celebration could not be put into old dry wineskins of asceticism that would burst under the pressure.

A STREET LADY FINDS A NEW HOME AND PEACE

The meaning of forgiveness is so important for Luke that he devotes one of his longest stories to illustrate its meaning. He omits the story of the woman at Bethany in Mark and Matthew just before Jesus' passion, but takes many details of those stories and places them in his account of the penitent woman.

One of the Pharisees asked Jesus to eat with him, and he went into the Pharisee's house and took his place at the table. And a woman in the city, who was a sinner, having learned that he was eating in the Pharisee's house, brought an alabaster jar of ointment. She stood behind him at his feet, weeping, and began to bathe his feet with her tears and to dry them with her hair. Then she continued kissing his feet and anointing them with the ointment (7:36-38).

The contrast between the Pharisee and the woman is evident. He is a respected religious leader and it is an honor to be invited to his house. On the other hand, a woman of doubtful reputation enters the house and places herself at Jesus' feet. The Pharisee, of course, would not even be seen with such a person. Her entry into his house was almost like the desecration of a holy place. Women often did perform the usual roles of hospitality, such as washing the feet and anointing with oil. However, this woman's actions were extravagant and very affectionate. She was crying with deep emotion, unable to speak, and washed Jesus' feet with her tears. She even let down her own hair, a symbol of self giving. Then she used her hair as a towel to dry Jesus' feet which she kissed not just once but many times. Finally she anointed his feet with precious ointment.

The shocked Pharisee noticed every detail and said to himself, "If this man were a prophet, he would have known who and what kind of woman this is who is touching him—that she is a sinner" (7:39). Ironically, Jesus sees this in reverse. He knows that the "disreputable" woman is really a holy person and the Pharisee is the sinner. Jesus then illustrates this with a parable about two people who were forgiven considerable debts, one of fifty *denarii* and the other, five hundred *denarii*. Jesus asked Simon which would love the creditor more. Simon answered, "I suppose the one for whom he canceled the greater debt."

Jesus then applied the parable to the woman and Simon. The key is the verb for "forgive" or "cancel" that Luke has here. It is from the root *charis*, meaning grace or favor. God's loving favor is the cause of forgiveness and has prompted the affectionate response shown by the woman. This shows that she has really experienced forgiveness. Jesus notes that Simon had not offered the usual signs of hospitality: an embrace, a kiss, and the washing of feet. Perhaps he wanted to play it safe and avoid the criticism of those who saw Jesus as an associate of tax collectors and sinners. Hospitality is more than external and means taking a person in to share the intimacy of the family. Simon did not feel he needed Jesus' forgiving presence into his house because he was already a just man.

In contrast, this woman supplied the kiss of welcome in a most affectionate and total way. She offered hospitality to Jesus *in the house of her inner self.* So Jesus tells the others, "Therefore, I tell you, her sins, which were many, have been forgiven; hence she has shown great love. But the one to whom little is forgiven, loves little" (7:47). Jesus then told her, "Your sins are forgiven" just as he told the paralytic previously. Finally he said to her, "Your faith has saved you; go in *peace.*" The verb "save" indicates here a restoration to wholeness and harmony which is the meaning of peace. A peace greeting was usually given not only upon arrival but at departure. So Jesus returns the greeting, kiss, and embrace of peace that she had given to him.

PARABLES OF PEACE, *METANOIA*, AND FORGIVENESS

Luke has a series of three parables in 15:1-32 which he introduces with the Pharisees' and scribes' criticism, "This fellow welcomes sinners and eats with them." The three parables have a definite similar fourfold literary pattern: (1) A tragic loss in the form of a lost sheep, a lost coin, or a lost son. (2) A continued search in the forms of a shepherd for the sheep, a woman sweeping the entire house for a coin, the father looking down the road every day for his son. (3) A repeated joyful *eureka* theme. (4) A community celebration, the shepherd or woman with their friends or a party dinner for the lost son with music and dancing.

The first parable over the lost sheep reflects the biblical concern for lost or stray animals found in the Torah. However, it is not a matter of simply abandoning the other ninety-nine. Jesus declares, "I tell you, there will be more joy in heaven over one sinner who repents than over ninety-nine righteous persons who need no repentance" (15:7). The contrast is between the ninety-nine *who need no repentance* and the one sinner who *repents*. Joy and rejoicing accompany all three parables, five times mentioned in the first two, while the third has a party atmosphere. Sin is certainly sad, but repentance should be joyful.

All three parables present the importance of even one person who has this *metanoia*. The first two repeat the same phrase at the end, "over one sinner" (15:7, 10). This concern for even one person is a special quality of Jesus' in Luke. In the third parable of the lost son, the father also goes out separately to the angered son. Jesus also has individual calls to Levi, the tax collector, and Zacchaeus, the chief tax official. It is Jesus' special look toward Peter that brings him to repentance (22:61). Even on the cross while dying, Jesus turns to pardon one of those crucified at his side.

THE PARABLE OF THE PRODIGAL FATHER

The third parable brings out special qualities of *metanoia* that need to be examined more in detail. The parable is commonly called the "Prodigal Son," but "Prodigal Father" better reflects a dictionary meaning of lavish or superabundant, sometimes on the reckless side. The story begins with the simple statement: "There was a man who had two sons. The younger of them said to his father, 'Father, give me the share of the property that will belong to me.' So he divided his property between them" (15:11-12). Even the Bible questions the wisdom of a father's decision to give away an inheritance to a young son: Sirach writes, "To son or wife, to brother or friend, do not give power over yourself, as long as you live; and do not give your property to another, in case you change your mind and must ask for it" (33:20). So we are dealing with a "foolish parent" according to human standards which are quite different from God's.

The worst expectations of any parent follow: The young man soon left home with this bonanza and quickly spent it all on riotous living. Soon he was reduced to dire poverty and was forced to even accept a job feeding pigs. Nothing could be lower than this for a Jew and there is a hint that he has even abandoned his religion also. However, in the depths of despair "he came to himself," recalled his home and parents and set off to return.

> So he set off and went to his father. But while he was still far off, his father saw him and was filled with compassion; he ran and put his arms around him and kissed him (15:20).

Here we find the first steps toward *metanoia*. The son "comes to himself" but this is accompanied by the image of loving parents (both of whom represented by the father, who in turn stands for God). The image is based on reality as the father had been watching every day down the road, hoping his wayward son would return. This is why he saw him from a distance. Then he did what the younger person should have done: he actually ran toward him and took the initiative to welcome him with an embrace and kiss of peace.

However, what is central are the inner feelings of the father. "He was filled with compassion, *esplangnisthē*." We will later study this word in the next chapter as connected to Jesus' statement in the Sermon on the Mount, "Be merciful, just as your Father is merciful" (6:36). Zechariah announced that his son John would "guide our feet in the way of peace" because of the inner *splangchna*, the visceral or gut feelings of God (1:78-79). This is rooted in the revelation of God's greatest inner quality, his *rachum*, womb compassion, from the root *rechem*, meaning womb.

The next step in *metanoia* is full restoration to the family with a joyful meal and celebration enhanced by hiring musicians and dancers. The great center dish was the fatted calf mentioned four times. Meat was not eaten that often and reserved for special occasions. With no refrigeration available, this special calf was kept near the home and nourished with the best food. When all was prepared they began to celebrate. But one person was missing, the elder brother. He had been working hard as usual in the fields and when he heard the party music was for his brother, he was so angry that he refused to go in. He could not bear the thought of going in to give his brother a welcome home with the usual greeting of peace, an embrace and a kiss.

At this point, the father, in his compassion goes out to talk with him, just as he took the initiative with the younger son. The father first let the elder son express his anger. After all he had worked faithfully for so many years without such a party for him and his friends. And now all this for someone who had "devoured your property with prostitutes." The father then expressed his understanding with these words, "Son, you are always with me, and all that is mine is yours. But we had to celebrate and rejoice, because this brother of yours was dead and has come to life; he was lost and has been found" (15:32).

In writing his story Luke has the father as the principal character because of the symbolism of God. Yet the father acts with the feminine divine attribute of *rachum*. It is very likely that Luke was influenced by the story in the book of Tobias (5:14). Tobias was not a prodigal son, but he had delayed his return from a journey because of arrangements for his marriage. Consequently his parents were very worried about him. The text reads that Anna, Tobias's mother "sat looking intently down the road by which her son would come." Then, when she caught sight of him, she said to her husband (who was blind), "Look, your son is coming." Finally, she *ran* up to her son and *put her arms around him*, saying, "Now that I have seen you my child, I am ready to die."

WHAT TO DO ABOUT BACKSLIDERS?

On one occasion, Jesus said, "Be on your guard! If another disciple sins, you must rebuke the offender, and if there is repentance, you must forgive. And if the same person sins against you seven times a day, and turns back to you seven times and says, 'I repent,' you must forgive" (17:3-4). In Matthew there is a similar saying when Peter asks Jesus how often he should forgive his brother—seven times? Jesus answers that it should not be seven times but seventy-seven times" (Matt 18:21-23). Luke seems to "correct" a possible misunderstanding of Matthew's version by adding twice the words, "I repent." There must be a genuine wish to change before there can be real forgiveness and reconciliation. However, there are "little ones" whom Jesus has just mentioned (17:2) who do have sincere goodwill but fall again and again like little children learning to walk. Thus real forgiveness is an act in progress that must be patiently renewed in a real spirit of compassion followed by restoration of relationships.

SUMMARY

Luke is the feature Gospel of forgiveness and *metanoia*. He often either has both together or adds *metanoia* to stories of forgiveness. Jesus assures the gospel audience that he has "power on earth to forgive sins" in the story of the paralytic's cure. This becomes immediately applied to popular enemies such as tax collectors and sinners, with the additional requirement of *metanoia*. Following this, the joyful character of forgiveness is shown in the similitude to a wedding feast and new wine. Luke uses the occasion of the forgiveness of a sinful woman to provide an example of full restoration to the joy, peace, and affection of a family relationship with Jesus. Three parables in chapter 15 provide teachings on the essential qualities of *metanoia* and forgiveness. Among these are the initiative and compassion of God, the spirit of joy, community restoration, and celebration, along with special attention to each individual.

COROLLARY FOR TODAY

As in the time of Jesus, there are vast fringe areas of society that ordinary "religious people" do not come in contact with. These became the special concern of Jesus' ministry and must be also embraced by his genuine followers. As in Jesus' life and parables, the first step is the inner womb-compassion of God that is experienced when believers take the initiative to be exposed to and moved by those who are most in need of spiritual as well as physical help. With Jesus this was never through "mass production" but by close individual contact and friendship with those who feel abandoned and neglected. The gospel stories of forgiveness and *metanoia* remind us that this is often a daily experience of renewal and not a once and for all occurrence.

6

The Sermon on the Plain: Part I. Roots

IN MATTHEW'S SERMON ON THE MOUNTAIN, JESUS IS SEATED ON A mountaintop like Moses who received the Ten Commandments from God. In Luke, Jesus comes down from the mount to a level plain so he can speak directly to his disciples and a large audience for every time and place. Luke's version is much shorter and omits all references to the Law or Scriptures so the summary of Jesus' teachings can reach everyone in the world. The evangelist wants to show that Jesus' teaching and example provides a way that his disciples can be always recognized by practicing virtues even superior to those much esteemed in the Greek world.

A look at the sermon's context highlights the special place it has in Luke's Gospel. Previously, Luke described several conflicts between Jesus and religious leaders over the meaning of the Sabbath. In all of these, Jesus stated the priority of sensitivity for human need over the letter of the Sabbath rest laws. At the end of these stories, the leaders "were filled with fury and discussed with one another what they might do to Jesus' (6:11). In this foreshadowing atmosphere of his death, Jesus looks to the future and the continuation of his mission through his disciples.

As a result, he went away to pray all night on a mountain before deciding to choose twelve apostles as his special successors

(6:12). At daybreak he called his disciples and selected the twelve names that Luke records. Then together with them, Jesus came down to the level plain. There a large crowd, even from far-away places joined with the disciples to listen to Jesus' instruction. So the Sermon in Luke is a special testament of teaching that Jesus wishes to hand down to his disciples and the world.

THE CORE OF THE SERMON: IMITATION OF GOD

In Jewish piety the highest place was given to imitation of God. This *Imitatio Dei* later became the summit of Christian spirituality. Jesus bases his instructions on this ideal with the words: "Be merciful as your Father is merciful" (6:36). This *mercy* is the supreme divine attribute that God revealed to Moses, his *rachum,* or inner womb compassion, from the root *rechem,* meaning "womb" (Exod 34:6). For "merciful" in the above quotation, Luke has the plural of the Greek *oiktirmōn.* This verbal-noun emphasizes the inner-felt quality of mercy. Only Luke among the Gospels has it once in this place only. It is the same word used in the Greek Septuagint Bible translation of *rachum* in the revelation of the meaning of God's attributes in Exodus 34:6 and 33:17. Confirming the connection, St. Paul quotes the same incident in Romans 9:14 by writing, "He [God] says to Moses, 'I will have compassion upon whom I will have compassion'" (the same root, *oikteireō*). So we must turn to this unique revelation in Exodus to find the roots of Jesus' statement to be merciful as the Father.

THE REVELATION OF THE INNER *RACHUM* QUALITY OF GOD'S NAME

At the burning bush at Sinai, God had revealed his name YHWH to Moses (Exod 3:14). However, in the course of time, out of reverence this sacred name was rarely pronounced. Instead, a substitute, *Adonai,* "LORD," was read instead whenever the divine name appeared in the text. In the English Bible we have LORD, usually in capital letters to signify this. It will appear over six thousand times. Under this powerful name, God led his people out of Egypt, across the Red Sea, and to Mount Sinai. There Moses climbed the mountain to receive the covenant declaration of the Ten Commandments from God. However, when Moses came down from the mountain he found that the people, impatient for his return, were worshiping the image of a golden calf. In anger, Moses broke the stone tablets and punished those responsible. At this point God told Moses he would no longer guide his people to the promised land but would send an angel instead.

However, God's apparent refusal was only meant to push Moses to appeal to the forgiving merciful attributes of YHWH. In reply to Moses, God promised him he would pass by and reveal the meaning of his name while Moses hid nearby in a rock cleft. Accordingly, the Lord descended and passed by him proclaiming, "The LORD (YHWH), the LORD (YHWH), a God merciful and gracious, slow to anger and abounding in steadfast love and faithfulness . . . forgiving iniquity and transgression and sin" (Exod 34:6). This "merciful" is *rachum* in Hebrew, from the root *rechem,* "womb." This primary feminine quality is a deep-felt womb-compassionate love bringing forgiveness, even when the covenant tablets had been disregarded and destroyed. As a result, God agreed to renew his covenant and once again accompany his people to the Promised Land.

In the text above, the first and greatest description of YHWH's name lies behind the word *rachum,* "merciful." The meaning is rooted in its source in a mother's womb. The Bible portrays the womb as the root location for the beginnings of love. It is where a mother feels the deepest human love, that for a child. Likewise, the first experience of love for a child begins in the womb with the perception of a mother's nourishing care poured out from her heart through the throbbing umbilical chord. This is the distinctly feminine aspect of YHWH's loving nature. The noun *rachum* is found fifty-seven times in the Scriptures and the verb around fifty times. It stands as the primary attribute of God's nature. Human beings first knew this in the womb where they experienced God at work in such a miraculous manner. Although feminine in origin, the word is used in a broader range of meaning.

THE BEGINNING OF GOD'S *RACHUM* ACTIVITY IN HUMAN LIFE

To understand this better, we need to look at biblical descriptions of the beginning and formation of life. In the birth process, God begins to work in the dark unseen recesses of a mother's womb. In the Genesis account, "The man named his wife Eve because she was the mother of all the living" (3:20). This is a popular etymology based on the similarity of her name in Hebrew with the word for life. The early, pre-Christian Greek Bible translation takes this up by noting that her name was *zōē*, "life," because she was the mother of all the living. The Bible focuses on the womb as the special workshop of God. The word *rechem* is found eighty-six times in the Bible. The birth of a first child, as the opening marvel of God's work is a cause for special joy. The firstborn is then dedicated to God in a special way. Originally, the firstborn son was offered to God as a priest.

Many Scripture passages describe God's creative activity in the womb. The birth of the very first child in the Bible is given special attention as an extraordinary event: "Now the man knew his wife Eve, and she conceived and bore Cain, saying, 'I have brought forth a man with the help of the LORD'" (4:1). According to biblical custom, a name often commemorates an event. In this case, the son's name, Cain, is a play on the words, "bring forth" or "produce." The Psalmist was filled with wonder about this inner activity in the womb as he prays to God:

It was you who formed my inward parts; you knit me together in my mother's womb. I praise you for I am fearfully and wonderfully made. Wonderful are your works; that I know very well. My frame was not hidden from you, when I was being made in secret, intricately woven in the depths of the earth. Your eyes

beheld my unformed substance. In your book were written all
the days that were formed for me, when none of them yet ex-
isted. How weighty to me are your thoughts, O God, how vast
the sum of them (139:13-17).

The description of the Psalmist parallels the creation story.
The womb is compared to earth: "My frame was not hidden
from you . . . intricately woven in the depths of the earth." In
the creation narrative, God formed the first human being from
the dust of the earth (2:7). The name "Adam" in Hebrew is taken
from the word *Adamah*, which means earth. The book of Wisdom echoes the connection between earth and womb when the
writer declares: "I also am mortal, like everyone else, a descendant of the first-formed child of earth; and in the womb of a
mother I was molded into flesh" (7:1).

The book of Job describes the womb as the place of God's
special creativity: "Did not he who made me in the womb make
them? And did not one fashion us in the womb?" (31:15). Isaiah
writes, "Thus says the LORD who made you, who formed you in
the womb and will help you" (44:2, 24). Because of this intimate
bond of mother and child, God speaks through Isaiah, "Can a
woman forget her nursing child, or show no compassion for the
child of her womb?" (49:15). For this reason, the highest quality
of God's love is expressed in the word *rachum*, compassion love.

THE CONJUNCTION OF THE WOMB
AND HEART IMAGE

The biblical appreciation of this imagery is founded on the
deep psychological experience of every child during the first nine
months of existence. The womb is like a dark water bed where
there are two great rhythms, those of mother's breathing and
those of her heartbeat. In the first of these, the watery envelope
within the womb compressed and expanded with her every
breath. This movement also shook and moved the embryo in un-
derwater aerobics. Between the two rhythms of breath and

heartbeat, we led a "rock-and-roll" existence even before our feet could dance. The nine-month sojourn in this "hot tub" gave us a music appreciation course that would never be forgotten.

The ancients did not know the scientific components of air. But they were keenly aware that blood was the carrier and transmitter of life/air and that the central point of transfer was the heart. The traditional Hebrew and Jewish conviction about the sacredness of blood was founded on the belief that life within the blood was a direct gift from the Creator. They knew also that the umbilical cord carried this blood from the heart to the womb.

The profound influence of mother's heartbeat, experienced through the throbbing umbilical cord, can be illustrated by a few observations. Our first nine months were dominated by this incessant heart throb. This was a total experience as each pulsating motion of the umbilical cord shook the watery capsule in the womb. Some of the figures are amazing. The average maternal heartbeat is about 60 beats a minute. This comes to about 3,600 an hour, 84,699 a day, and close to 24 million during the time of gestation. In the womb, we could sense when mother's heartbeat slowed during sleep to 40 to 50 a minute and then we rested also. We also experienced when mother was excited and the heart rhythm speeded up. That stimulated our own excitement as well. During this whole time a most powerful eidetic (very vivid) image of the heart was being formed in the unconscious.

After birth this eidetic heart image continued to grow in early months, especially when there were hours of nursing each day. The womb experience was prolonged as the infant pressed against mother's breast and sensed the continuation of the maternal heartbeat. Observation and studies show that a child shows a preference for mother's left side because the heart beat is better felt there. Even outside of nursing time, tests have shown that infants exposed to a human heart's sound cry less and gain weight faster. Today, even business has commercialized this finding by equipping cribs with heartbeat simulators for under the baby's pillow. The mechanisms are accompanied with guarantees that baby will cry less, gain weight better, and be more content. When I talked about this once to a nurse, she told me about an old secret used by nurses long ago. This was to place an alarm clock under crib pillows to achieve the same effect. Instinct often precedes scientific studies.

The nursing or holding of the child actually prolonged and increased the womb/heart experience. The womb perception was essentially tactile, but in mother's bosom the auditory effect amplified its experience. The watery atmosphere of the womb envelope continued with the liquid nourishment of mother's milk. In addition, the first visual image of a mother from the limited sight of a newborn was the mother's breast from which a precious white elixir of life flowed. My wife told me once that she believed that the visual heart image we possess comes from mother's breasts, rather than the physical heart that few people ever see.

The Bible puts together breasts and womb as combining to form an image of God's special creative activity. Jacob gave a final blessing to his son Joseph asking that God would bless him, "With the blessings of heaven above, blessings of the deep that lies beneath, blessings of the breast and blessings of the womb" (Gen 49:25). In effect, this was telling a man that his greatest blessing was his fruitful wife. On one occasion, while Jesus was speaking, "A woman in the crowd raised her voice and said to him, 'Blessed is the womb that bore you and the breasts that nursed you!'" But Jesus replied, "Blessed rather are those who hear the word of God and keep it" (Luke 11:27-28). In saying this, Jesus was drawing attention to the Word of God which also goes into the womb/heart in the parable of the seed (Luke 8:5-11). There it can be nourished and grow until it produces a hundredfold harvest.

LUKE: HEART, WOMB, AND *SPLANGCHNA* IN GOD, JESUS, AND HUMANS

Luke could be called the "gospel of the heart," since the word is found twenty-four times in his Gospel—more than in any other. By way of example, the heart preeminence begins with the mission of the Baptist to "turn the hearts of parents to their children" (1:17). Mary is the example of those who ponder over words and events in her heart (2:19). In the Sermon on the Plain the importance of the heart as the source of intentions, words, and actions is mentioned three times. In the seed parable, the seed that falls into a good heart produces a hundredfold miraculous harvest (8:12). In the concluding journey of the disciples to Emmaus, the words of the mysterious stranger, Jesus in disguise, penetrate so deeply that the disciples later reflect, "Were not our hearts burning within us?" (24:32).

The Acts of the Apostles, Luke's second volume, continues the heart focus, mentioning it twenty-one times. For example, he describes the early Jerusalem community as being "of one heart and soul," as they shared their food and goods with one another (Acts 4:32-35). Lydia of Philippi and others became converts because "The Lord opened her heart to listen eagerly to what was said by Paul" (16:14). The book closes with a quotation from Isaiah to explain that the differing responses to Paul's preaching are matters of the heart (Acts 28:26-27).

Heart, womb, and *splangchna* are all interconnected in Luke. We have already seen in chapter 3 how Zechariah predicted that his son the Baptist would accomplish his mission through the "tender mercy *(splangchna)* of our God" (1:78). This Greek word refers to the viscera, or inner gut feelings of the abdomen, which are in turn connected to the heart through the aorta. The connected feelings are relayed along the splanchnic nerve that runs beside the aorta from the heart to the abdomen. So we are dealing with a felt reality whose feelings are transferred by a special nerve, whose name is well known in modern medical and scientific terminology and whose definition is found in the dictionary under "splanchnic."

In the Sermon on the Plain, we have seen above that Luke has the word "merciful," *oiktirmōn* in writing, "Be merciful just as your Father is merciful" (6:36). He does not use it elsewhere perhaps because of its unique quality. Instead, he will build on the parallel root *splangchna*, beginning as we have seen with Zachary's *Benedictus.* However, the interconnection of *splang-*

chna and *oiktireō* is found in the Letter of James where the author states that the Lord is compassionate—*polysplangchnos* and merciful, *oiktirmōn* (5:11).

JESUS, THE DIVINE VISITOR ACTS LIKE GOD THROUGH THIS MERCY—*SPLANGCHNA*

Here we can note several examples. Jesus visits the town of Naim, a story which Luke relates in typical dramatic fashion. As Jesus and his disciples near the town gate, he meets a departing procession caused by the greatest tragedy that can face a human being: the death of the only young son of a widow. As Jesus nears the funeral pall, he would be expected to join them and walk with them to the cemetery. Instead, he takes in deeply the whole pathos. He was moved with compassion, *esplangchnisthē*. Then he ordered the procession of death to stop and touched the pall, which would ordinarily bring upon him the ritual impurity of death. Instead, his touch brings new life as the young man sits up and begins to talk. With a gesture of kindness, Jesus restores him to his mother. The crowd at Naim was overcome with fear and exclaimed, "A great prophet has risen among us" and *"God has visited his people"* (7:16). This word went out to the whole region.

The parable of the Good Samaritan really illustrates Jesus' own loving initiative. An unknown stranger was traveling down the winding dangerous road from Jerusalem to Jericho. A band of robbers ambushed him around a road bend. "They stripped him, beat him, and went away, leaving him half dead" (10:31). A priest and then a Levite soon came down the road. In each case they saw the victim from some distance but took care not to get too near by deliberately *passing by on the other side of the road*. Some time later a traveling Samaritan, regarded as a foreigner, came along and risked to *come near* the unfortunate victim. As a result, he was moved with compassion, *esplangchnisthē*. This prompted him to take every possible means to help, even at risk to himself. At the end of the parable, Jesus' advice to the gospel audience is "Go and do likewise" (10:37). Here the divine *splangchna* or mercy works even through someone traditionally regarded as an enemy.

Another parable applies the splanchnic theme to forgiveness. A young son demanded his share of his parents' inheritance and went off to a foreign country where he squandered everything. He was finally reduced to the most shameful occupation for a Jew, that of feeding pigs for Gentile owners. Finally, he woke up to what had happened to his life, remembered his parents' love and decided to return home. His father too (representing God) was thinking of him at the same time. Every day he watched the road for some sign of his son in the distance. One day he spotted the boy afar off and was moved with compassion, *esplangchnisthē*.

This deep inner feeling prompted the father to run "foolishly" to his son, put his arms around him and kiss him. Not only that— he even arranged the greatest party ever seen in those parts. He brought new clothes for his son, hired an orchestra with dancers, and prepared a sumptuous meal. The fatted calf (mentioned four times), reserved for extraordinary occasions, was brought out and roasted. The attitude of the elder son on seeing all this represents those of the gospel audience who might think, "What about us who have always been faithful?" The Father can only reply, "Son, you are always with me and all that is mine is yours. But we had to celebrate and rejoice, because this brother of yours was dead and has come to life; he was lost and has been found" (15:31-32).

THE PASSIVE QUALITY OF
THE DIVINE *SPLANCHNIC* ACTION

In each case above we notice that God or human beings are moved by first paying sensitive, careful attention. At Naim, the text literally reads that *"seeing her,* the Lord was moved to compassion" (7:13). In the Good Samaritan parable, there is a sharp contrast: Both the priest and Levite did not want to come close to the wounded man to absorb the full impact of what had happened, but passed deliberately on the other side of the road. However the Samaritan *came near him* and was deeply moved

(10:33). The father of the prodigal son watched the road each day ready to be moved by his son's need (15:20). Consequently, love does not flow from an act of the will, but from deliberately leaving one's self open and vulnerable to the need of others.

This was true of God before he revealed his name to Moses near Sinai at the burning bush (Exod 3:13-15). God said that he had *heard* the cries of his people and *looked upon* their afflictions. This is what moved him to act. Later at Sinai, God changed his mind about leaving his people after the heart rending plea of Moses and then revealed the meaning of the divine name.

SUMMARY

In the Sermon on the Plain, Jesus reveals that the highest act of a human being is to imitate God as a merciful Father. This attribute of mercy is that of *rachum*, a womb-compassion, coming from the Hebrew root *rechem*, "womb." God revealed this quality to Moses when he requested a special vision of God's nature after the people had broken the covenant at Mount Sinai. Luke translates this compassion, or mercy as *oiktirmōn*. As a "gospel of the heart" Luke is especially concerned about these womb/heart feelings which have their roots in the beginning of life in the womb. The evangelist describes Jesus, like God, as reacting to human need through his *splangchna* or "gut feelings" that proceed from the heart and womb. He also presents the Good Samaritan as a human being, even as a stereotyped enemy acting in the same fashion. In a parable of forgiveness the father of the prodigal son also exhibits this quality through his search, restoration, and renewal of his lost son.

COROLLARY FOR TODAY

The mercy described in the Sermon on the Plain does not flow from the mind or willpower but through being drawn out from someone by their willingness to expose themselves and be touched by the pain, misery, or need of others. Human beings

share with God this wonderful divine quality of mercy, *rachum*.
Yet it is deep within and cannot be elicited except through the
practice of deep sensitivity not only to other human beings, but
to animals and all creatures. The will, however, does have a part
to play. By making the choice to expose ourselves to others' needs,
and not "pass by on the other side" as in the Samaritan story the
door becomes open to becoming truly like God in his (or better
"her," because of the womb-like quality!) highest attribute.

7

The Sermon on the Plain: Part II. Practices

LUKE HAS CAREFULLY SET THE ATMOSPHERE OF THE SERMON ON THE Plain. A great crowd from far-off places came to Jesus where they joined with his disciples. They had come to hear him and be healed of their sicknesses. Everyone was trying to touch him for "power came out from him and healed all of them" (6:19). Thus Jesus' own actions and power set the source and example for his teachings. As a special preface, Luke writes, "Then he *looked up* at his disciples and said. . . ." The direct glance at his followers shows that the teachings are especially for them as his own special testament. Therefore his power will make it possible for them to follow them.

LOVE OF ENEMIES AND NONVIOLENT POSITIVE RESPONSE TO INJURY

The beatitudes are an introduction to Jesus' teachings. We have already discussed in chapter 4 the justice context in the contrasts between rich and poor. However, there is a direction of audience change beginning in verse 27 with the words: "But I say to you that listen" and continuing with "Love your enemies. . . ." These appear to be directed to a broader audience than previously with the beatitudes where Jesus looked up to his disciples and spoke (6:20). The teachings that follow in verses 27-49 are universal and could appeal to any audience, even regardless of their religion. They are a short summary of twenty verses that could be easily memorized and used as a challenge to address any audience in the Greek world, or even today.

The above verses are preceded by sharp preceding statements on hatred and opposition to prepare for Jesus' core teachings that follow in regard to love of enemies. The first is,

> Blessed are you when people hate you, and when they exclude you, revile you, and defame you on account of the Son of Man. Rejoice in that day and leap for joy, for surely your reward is great in heaven; for that is what their ancestors did to the prophets (6:22-23).

> Woe to you when all speak well of you, for that is what their ancestors did to the false prophets (6:26).

Jesus' teaching is unlike false prophets of the past who carefully chose to say what pleased people and brought popularity. In contrast, Jesus will speak the truth and that will often result in hatred and opposition. However this will not be just personal. Since the truth comes from God, it will have God's blessing and thus be the occasion of rejoicing and dancing as well as special rewards. By way of contrast to false prophets and enemies, Jesus states, "But I say to you that listen, 'Love your enemies . . . '" (6:27). This is Jesus' special teaching on love for enemies that is repeated again in 6:35.

The question of reconciliation with enemies will also extend to other areas in this Gospel, as we will see in coming chapters. We have noted that even hated tax collectors and soldiers come to John for baptism (3:13-14). It seems deliberate on Luke's part that right after Jesus' sermon, a Roman centurion, the greatest symbol of harsh oppression, appears on the scene and sends messengers to ask Jesus to cure his servant. Jesus is even willing to go to his house to do so, but the centurion humbly trusts that the cure can take place even from a distance. The Samaritans are traditional enemies of the Jews who even refused Jesus hospitality on his journey to Jerusalem (9:51-56). His disciples James and John were so angry about this that they wanted to call down lightning from heaven to destroy them. But Jesus turned and rebuked them for their attitude. Later a Samaritan even becomes the model for how a true believer should act in regard to those in need.

"Love your enemies, do good to those who hate you, bless those who curse you, pray for those who abuse [persecute] you" (6:27).

Matthew's Sermon on the Mount goes as far as directing prayer for persecutors (5:44), but Luke's version takes a giant step further. Jesus asks specifically for doing good to enemies. There is no question of passive acceptance or resignation; it is active response to evil and evil-doers in a surprising way. Jesus' teaching is a mirror of his own actions. On the cross he prays for those who are torturing and killing him (24:34). He prays for Simon Peter at his last supper for he knows he will give in to human weakness and betray him (22:31). Jesus turns and looks to Peter after he betrayed him as an invitation to reconciliation. Even to Judas, Jesus extends hope by saying to him when he approached for his arrest, "Is it with a kiss that you are betraying the Son of Man?" (22:47). As for "doing good to enemies," Jesus even healed the ear of one of his attackers who had suffered injury by the sword of one of his disciples (22:50).

"Bless those who curse you." A curse was regarded as an effective way of hurting others by invoking the worst punishments of God. The ancient world very much feared "bad vibrations" of this kind. To reverse this damage by a kind blessing to share benevolent divine energy would be a great disarming surprise. This was not just an imaginary ideal but something to be put in practice by traveling apostles. St. Paul wrote to the Corinthians about how he responded to such curses: "When reviled we bless; when persecuted we endure; when slandered we speak kindly" (1 Cor 4:12-13).

It is interesting to note that even St. Paul did not always rise to such heights. When he was on trial before the council, the high priest Ananias ordered him to be struck on the mouth. This was not only painful but especially insulting. To this Paul responded with a curse, "God will strike you, you whitewashed wall! Are you sitting there to judge me according to the law, and yet in violation of the law you order me to be struck?" (Acts 23:3). Some of the bystanders then accused Paul of insulting the high priest. To his credit, Paul apologized, "I did not realize, brothers, that he was high priest; for it is written, 'You shall not speak evil of a leader of your people.'"

"Pray for those who persecute you." The people who occupy our thoughts are both those whom we love and those who hurt us. So there is an automatic reminder to pray for those who invade even our minds.

> If anyone strikes you on the cheek, offer the other also; and from anyone who takes away your coat do not withhold even your shirt. Give to everyone who begs from you; and if anyone takes away your goods, do not ask for them again (6:29-30).

"Turning the other cheek" has become over the centuries a hyperbolic expression for preferring even a second injury to responding with violence. A strike on the face or cheek, like that of St. Paul above was a shameful insult that would move the average person to prompt retaliation to preserve their sense of honor. A coat or cloak was the outer garment, which could be taken away either by theft or as a security for a loan. But the shirt or tunic was immediately over the skin, so to take that away would leave a person completely naked. This is a humorous reprisal by offering even more to someone violently taking one's clothes away. Importunate beggars following people around to shame them would ordinarily prompt an angry dismissal. Instead they are treated with generous and cheerful giving. This changes what is practically a robbery into a loving gift. The whole tenor or these sayings is that of overcoming evil with cheerful, good actions.

"Do to others as you would have them do to you" (6:31) is a summary well known as the Golden Rule. However the expression does not regard self-love as a criterion but views the self as the cherished image of God at creation (Gen 1:26). This summary is so important that Luke has it a second time when a lawyer asks Jesus what must be done to gain eternal life. Jesus responds with the traditional *Shema* (Hear!) about loving God with one's whole heart, soul, mind, and heart (10:27). Then Luke does not add "you shall love your neighbor as yourself" as a second commandment, but joins it to the *Shema* so there is but one single commandment. Thus love of God and love of human beings are one and the same. This is illustrated by the parable of the Good Samaritan that follows.

The next section is meant to be a sharp contrast to the Greek ideal of friendship that for many had the characteristics of a good investment. Reciprocity, mutual loans, and advantageous business partnerships were hoped-for outcomes:

> If you love those who love you, what credit is that to you? For even sinners love those who love them. If you do good to those who do good to you, what credit is that to you? For even sinners do the same. If you lend to those from whom you hope to receive, what credit is that to you? Even sinners lend to sinners, to receive as much again (6:32-34).

However, Luke wants to show that Jesus' teaching goes far beyond Greek virtues. God's love as mirrored in human beings reaches out to all without ulterior motivation and without expectations of payoffs or gratitude.

> But love your enemies, do good, and lend, expecting nothing in return. Your reward will be great, and you will be children of the Most High; for he is kind to the ungrateful and the wicked. Be merciful, just as your Father is merciful (6:35-36).

Here, love of enemies is repeated again as the distinct quality of the love that Jesus teaches. This has a special reward from

God because it makes a person like God in the quality of that love. This is especially true of his mercy, which we have seen as his supreme quality of *rachum*, his womb-compassionate love. The subject of lending comes up for a second time. In chapter 4, on justice in Luke, the importance of forgiveness of debts was brought out, with reference to the Deuteronomy roots on debt forgiveness every seven years (15:1). To make sure that forgiveness of debts would not impede lending, Luke brings out the importance of lending even with limited hope of return.

WORDS, CONDEMNATION, AND DISPARAGEMENT OF OTHERS

Although Luke's Sermon is much shorter than that of Matthew, Luke gives more space and emphasis to this area. In a culture that is predominantly oral and not written, words and attitudes expressed by them have much more power and are communicated more widely. Thus they can have a large responsibility for creating enemies and setting up barriers to peace, reconciliation, and friendship.

> Do not judge, and you will not be judged; do not condemn, and you will not be condemned. Forgive, and you will be forgiven; give, and it will be given to you. A good measure, pressed down, shaken together, running over, will be put into your lap; for the measure you give will be the measure you get back (6:37-38).

In the text above, "judging" and "condemning" are in parallel and are almost the same. The words include the habit of derogatory remarks about others, finding fault, put-downs, carping, and the like. The contrast, "You will be judged or forgiven" involves the customary passive expression of avoiding God's name. The words expressed by people in regard to others often tell more about themselves than others and thus God will judge accordingly. On the positive side, a forgiving attitude shows the right disposition to being forgiven by God. However, this is not just tit-for-tat. God's forgiveness and true peace goes far beyond human practices. Thus it is not like the prevalent way of measuring grain at that time. The ordinary seller does not pack the grain down or fill it to an overflowing brim, but does just the opposite in giving the minimum.

Luke then brings this to application in regard to teachers, who often go beyond bounds in correcting others, rather than relying on their example. Jesus declares in a parable, "Can a blind person guide a blind person? Will not both fall into a pit? A disciple is not above the teacher, but everyone who is fully qualified will be like the teacher" (6:3). The concentration on changing others can result in treating them as objects, not people. Likewise, it makes teachers fail to see their own faults. So Jesus says,

> Why do you see the speck in your neighbor's eye, but do not notice the log in your own eye? Or how can you say to your neighbor, "Friend, let me take out the speck in your eye," when you yourself do not see the log in your own eye? You hypocrite, first take the log out of your own eye, and then you will see clearly to take the speck out of your neighbor's eye (6:41-42).

Jesus and the teachers in the early Church taught in a personal manner dealing with individuals and small groups. The contagion of good example is still the best way to inculcate virtue. Luke reinforces this by having Jesus give examples of a tree and its fruit and the contrast of a grape vine that produces thorns. Using Luke's favorite image of the heart, Jesus points out that meaningful words come from the "good treasure of the heart" (6:45). In Luke, Jesus concludes this by adding, "Why do you call me 'Lord, Lord,' and do not do what I tell you?" "Lord, Lord" was a repeated invocation of prayer. Yet even this means little if it does not emerge from the treasury of the heart which is open to Jesus' word and puts it into practice.

SUMMARY

The Sermon on the Plain is in itself a summary of action directives rooted on imitation of God's mercy. Love of enemies is the highest form of this imitation. Luke goes further than Matthew with very pointed action-based responses. Not just prayer but doing good to those who are hurtful whether through their words or actions. The motto of "do unto others" and identification with others' needs forms a valuable guide. Luke's Greek audience with their emphasis on the virtue of friendship are presented with Jesus' axioms for a supreme type of altruism that expects no return or payoff. Words of condemnation or judgment of others receive even more attention than in Matthew and merit God's own judgment in return. Forgiveness and positive words toward others are repaid by God in a superlative manner. Those called to teach and guide others should rely more on their example than constant correction that promotes blindness to one's own faults.

COROLLARY FOR TODAY

Jesus' words in the Sermon on the Plain are already brief summaries of his teaching in the entire Gospel. The concluding words call for coming to him, listening, and acting (6:47). Luke's advice for today's audience would be the same as that of Jesus after the parable of the Good Samaritan: "Go and do likewise" (10:37). It is especially interesting that the core statements in verses 27-49 are ecumenical in nature. They do not contain any credal statements. Even today they could be presented as a challenge to a new lifestyle that could be presented to an audience of different religions or even no religion at all.

8

"Love Your Enemies"

Response to Violence from a Gospel of Peace

LUKE TAKES SERIOUSLY JESUS' COMMAND TO LOVE ENEMIES RATHER than retaliate against them. In his Sermon on the Plain, Jesus does not provide theoretical ideals; he gives positive directions for action such as actively doing good for enemies, replying to their curses with blessings, and praying for them (6:27-28). Jesus encourages his disciples to develop a nonjudgmental attitude (6:37-42). Luke puts this in practice in the process of writing his own Gospel. The following areas may be taken as examples.

THREATS OF HELL, GEHENNA, OR ADVERSE JUDGMENT SHARPLY CURTAILED

In Matthew's Sermon on the Mount alone, fire, Gehenna, hell, or destruction is mentioned six times (5:22, 27, 30; 7:13, 19, 23). Luke's Sermon on the Plain has none of them. This model is reflected in the rest of Luke. As for fire, Luke shares with Matthew the warnings of the Baptist about fleeing from the wrath to come and the axe that lies at the root of a tree. Any tree without good fruit is to be cast into the fire (3:7-9; Matt 3:7-10). However these are warnings either for the crowds or Pharisees and scribes to accompany baptism with *metanoia*.

Luke has only two other references to fire or Gehenna as punishment in his Gospel: One of these is in the story of Lazarus (16:1-31) where the rich man complains about being tortured in flames. The other is advice not to fear enemies but God who has the power to cast into Gehenna (12:5). This contrasts with Matthew where Gehenna is mentioned seven times and in Mark, a much shorter Gospel, three. Both Matthew and Luke share the threat to Capernaum that the city will not be exalted to heaven and cast down into *Hades* (10:15; Matt 11:22). But *Hades* is a Greek term used for a "place for the dead" and does not necessarily imply punishment.

Outside the Sermon on the Mount, Matthew has six other references to the fire of judgment. Three are to fire or a furnace of fire in the parable of the weeds or net cast into the sea in chapter 13. Two more are punishments for scandal to little ones in 8:8-9. The last is the punishment of the accursed "into the eternal fire prepared for the devil and his angels" at the Last Judgment (25:41), which is called "eternal punishment" in 25:46. Luke omits all these and other threats of judgment in Matthew. For example, in the parable of good or evil things from the treasure of the heart, Luke omits the words, "I tell you, on the day of judgment you will have to give an account for every careless word you utter" (Matt 12:36; Luke 8:45). Also, in reference to shame before the Son of Man, Luke omits Matthew's words, "Then he [Son of Man] will repay everyone for what has been done" (16:27; Luke 9:26).

JESUS REBUKES BY PROXY
THE PROPHET ELIJAH FOR VIOLENCE

In the Hebrew Bible, King Ahaziah sent a captain with fifty soldiers to arrest Elijah (2 Kgs 1:9-12). The captain came to a hill where the prophet was seated and ordered him to promptly come down. But Elijah replied, "If I am a man of God, let fire come down from heaven and consume you and your fifty." Then fire (lightning) came down and destroyed the fifty soldiers. The king refused to believe this report and sent another captain with fifty more soldiers. The same dialog with Elijah occurred, and all fifty were struck by lightning. The king then sent a third captain with another armed troop. This time, the captain made a humble appeal to Elijah. Then the prophet, advised by an angel, agreed to accompany the captain to the king.

The above story has a comical twist on words and was likely meant to be a warning not to arrest or lay hands on a prophet guarded and protected by God. However, when Jesus went through Samaria on the way to Jerusalem, the Samaritans refused him hospitality (9:51-56). Then James and John recalled the story of Elijah as indicating the punishment for those mistreating a prophet in such an important matter. They said to Jesus, "Do you want us to command fire to come down from heaven and consume them?" (Some ancient Greek manuscripts make the reference to Elijah more explicit by adding, "As Elijah did.") Jesus then turned and rebuked James and John. Again, some ancient manuscripts make the rebuke more explicit by adding, "The Son of Man has not come to destroy the lives of human beings but to save them."

Luke's attitude toward violence is a likely reason why he omits some of the identification of John the Baptist with Elijah. Just before the Elijah story above, the text notes he was a "hairy man" and had a leather belt around him (2 Kgs 1:8). Both Matthew and Mark note the similarity of the Baptist's dress to Elijah (Matt 3:4; Mark 1:6), but Luke omits this. The same two Gospels have a reference to Elijah after Jesus' transfiguration. Matthew and Mark have a statement that Elijah has already come, which Matthew makes more explicit by stating that Jesus was speaking to them about the Baptist (17:13). Luke omits these. Luke also has no reference to Elijah's mention at the cross, as in Matthew and Mark.

RESPONSE TO THE HEROD FAMILY—THE WORST ENEMIES OF THE BAPTIST AND JESUS

Luke writes that the ministry of John the Baptist began when Herod (Antipas) was ruler of Galilee (3:1). The activity of the

Baptist and the throngs that came down to the Jordan to listen to him and receive baptism must have soon attracted Herod's attention. As a loyal puppet of Rome, Herod's first duty was to preserve the *Pax Romana* and to make sure that there were no dissenting or threatening messianic movements. Luke briefly notes that John was proclaiming good news to the people: "But Herod the ruler, who had been rebuked by him because of Herodias, his brother's wife, and because of all the evil things that Herod had done, added to them all by shutting up John in prison" (3:19).

The next we hear about Herod is that he was perplexed because he had heard about Jesus and his healings. Herod said, "John I beheaded; but who is this about whom I hear such things?" Then he tried to see him (9:9). Later we read that the Pharisees warned Jesus that Herod wanted to kill him. In reply, even Jesus could not restrain from referring to him as "that fox." Jesus then said that he would continue his work and healings because as a prophet he will not be killed outside of Jerusalem (13:32-34). Yet despite all this, Luke chooses not to report the extravagant violent scene reported by Matthew and Mark that Herod ordered the Baptist's head brought in as a banquet dish (Matt 14:1-2; Mark 6:14-29). Luke also does not describe the mass murder of babies around Bethlehem by Antipas's father, Herod the Great (Matt 2:16-18).

Herod the Great was indeed guilty of great atrocities, but Luke may have felt that this story was midrashic, influenced by the account of Pharaoh's actions at the birth of Moses (Exod 1:15-22). At the trial of Jesus, Pilate sent him to Herod who was in Jerusalem for the Passover. Jesus refused Herod's request for a sign or miracles and remained silent when Herod and his court treated him with contempt and put a royal cloak on him in mockery (23:6-12).

Following the Herod "tradition," Herod Agrippa I (A.D. 41–44), grandson of Herod the Great, tried to bring an early end to Christianity by killing James, the brother of John. Herod also arrested Peter and planned to kill him also at Passover (Acts 12:1-3). As a result of the constant prayer of the Church, Peter had a miraculous escape from prison and went to the house of Mary,

Mother of Mark, where the believers had gathered. After that "he left and went to another place" and Peter receives no further mention in Acts. The story of Herod's death is related by both Josephus, the historian, and Luke. A crowd of people hailed Herod as a god when he spoke to them but he failed to reject such a title and died a miserable death (12:20-33). Luke is content with this description and refrains from further disparaging him or the Herod family.

THE SOFTENING OF PUNISHMENTS FOR SIN
AND THE GRANTING OF NEW OPPORTUNITIES

Jesus curses a fig tree in Mark and Matthew symbolic of people's failure to produce fruits (Mark 11:12-14; Matt 21:18-22). Not only does Luke omit the fig tree curse but Jesus teaches a parable that a barren fig tree should be fertilized and given another opportunity. In this parable a man had patiently come to a fig tree for three years looking for fruit and then ordered his gardener to cut it down. But the gardener replied, "Sir, let it alone for one more year, until I dig around it and put manure on it. If it bears fruit next year, well and good; but if not, you can cut it down" (13:8-9).

In regard to repentance, Luke does not have Matthew's "three strike" program leading to excommunication. First, there is a one to one attempt; then there are two or three witnesses, and finally the whole Church. If the person does not listen they are to be regarded as outsiders, as if "a Gentile and tax collector" (18:15-17). Instead, Luke has, "Be on your guard! If another disciple sins, you must rebuke the offender, and if there is repentance, you must forgive. And if the same person sins against you seven times a day, and turns back to you seven times and says, 'I repent,' you must forgive" (17:3-4).

Both Matthew and Luke have the parable asking who is the faithful and prudent manager whom the master will put in charge of his slaves while he is away. If the manager sees that the master is delayed in returning and begins to beat his fellow slaves and get drunk, then the master will return and severely punish him (Matt 24:45-51). However, Luke's version adds a provision for those who were less serious offenders: "That slave who knew what his master wanted, but did not prepare himself or do what was wanted, will receive a severe beating. But the one who did not know and did what deserved a beating will receive a light beating. From everyone to whom much has been given, much will be required; and from the one to whom much has been entrusted, even more will be demanded" (12:47-48).

THE REVISION OF PARABLES OR STORIES TO ELIMINATE OR LESSEN VIOLENCE

The best example is the parable of the marriage feast (Matt 22:1-14). Here a king gave a wedding banquet for his son. Then he sent a slave to call those who were invited to his marriage feast, but they would not come. He then sends a second group to tell them that the meal is all prepared. But they all made light of it and went to their farms or other businesses. Some even seized the slaves and mistreated or even killed them. On hearing this, the king was enraged. He sent out his troops and destroyed the murderers and burnt their cities. Of course, this is a horrible wholesale retaliation.

In contrast, Luke has a similar parable, evidently from the same source as Matthew's (14:15-24). Here we have a great dinner to which someone invited many people. When dinner was ready, he sent out a notice for everyone to come. (In those days, with no refrigeration for meat; people had to come immediately when all was ready.) However, all the guests made various excuses and did not come. When the slaves returned and told this to their master, he was *angry* (as in Matthew's version). However, he does not likewise respond with retaliation, destruction, and murder. In accord with the principles of the Sermon on the Plain, he responds by actively doing good.

The master then shows even greater largesse by inviting more people, this time those most in need who could offer no return.

He told his slave, "Go out at once into the streets and lanes of the town and bring in the poor, the crippled, the blind, and the lame" (14:21). After they came, the slave told the master that there was still room. The master was anxious to have every possible guest at his dinner, so he even sent the slave to outsiders: "Go out into the roads and lanes, and compel people to come in, so that my house may be filled" (14:23).

The word "compel" has an unfortunate bad history of interpretation. In oriental ways of thinking it meant doing everything possible to show that a guest is welcome and simply must come. Since the parable is meant to be an image of God, Luke's version better accords with the principles of the Sermon on the Plain. There the ideal is love of enemies (6:27-28) shown by active good toward them and the model of imitating God—"Be merciful, just as your Father is merciful" (6:36).

The story of the cure of the centurion's servant is in both Matthew 8:5-13 and in Luke 7:1-10. Both accounts have a friendly view of the Roman and Jesus praises his faith. However, there is a decided difference in the attitude toward Israel. Matthew ends with a frightening picture of Israel's rejection in the words: "I tell you, many will come from east and west and will eat with Abraham and Isaac and Jacob in the kingdom of heaven, while the heirs of the kingdom will be thrown into the outer darkness, where there will be weeping and gnashing of teeth" (8:10-11).

Luke, however, omits these words and has similar ones in a different context where they refer to believers who thought they had automatic access to God's kingdom. Jesus says to them twice that he does not know them, even though they said, "We ate and drank with you, and you taught in our streets" (13:26). These people will be weeping when they see Abraham, Isaac, and Jacob as well as all the prophets in the kingdom of God but find themselves left out. Luke also introduced the centurion's story with a positive view of the Jewish people describing how the elders went to Jesus asking his help for the centurion. They said that he loved their people and had even built their synagogue for them (7:3-5).

The cleansing of the Temple has an important place in all the Gospels. However, Matthew and Mark present it in a much more violent way. Luke simply has, "Then he entered the temple and began to drive out those who were selling things there" (19:45). The other two Gospels have the cursing of a fig tree connected with it, symbolizing rejection of the people. Luke has none of this. Luke's description is very mild in comparison. There is no mention of the overturning of the money changers' tables or the seats of those who sold doves.

THE COSMIC COMBAT WITH SATAN
AND JESUS' RESPONSE

Luke's Gospel brings this out more than any other Gospel. He traces back the genealogy of Jesus to the beginning of the world with Adam "son of God" (3:23-38). This is immediately followed by Jesus' temptation by the devil in the desert. This makes a connection between the temptation and fall of Adam and Eve in paradise. In contrast, Matthew traces Jesus back to Abraham (1:1-17). The temptation story is not connected to it, but it occurs in 4:1-13 where it is more linked with the temptations of Israel in the desert. In late biblical history the temptation of the first parents was believed to be caused by Satan, working through the serpent. The book of Wisdom around the first century B.C. has the following: "Through the devil's envy, death entered the world, and those who belong to his company experience it" (2:24).

The New Testament accepted this connection. St. Paul wrote to the Corinthians advising them not to be astray, "as the serpent deceiving Eve by its cunning" (2 Cor 11:3). Here the devil is not explicitly mentioned but seems to be implied since Paul ends his advice by writing that "Satan disguises himself as an angel of light" (2 Cor 11:4). The book of Revelation has four citations connecting the devil and the serpent of Eden. It was also commonly accepted that death came into the world through submitting to the devil's temptation. The sin in the garden was one of pride and the desire of power. The serpent told Eve that when she ate the fruit she would be like the gods, knowing good and evil (Gen 3:5).

The temptations of Jesus are connected to the garden. The first is regarding food or bread, which we will see in chapter 13. The second treats of power; the third is that of recognition and glory. In the second temptation the devil showed Jesus all the kingdoms of the world in an instant. Then he said, "To you I will give their glory and all this authority; for it has been given over to me, and I give it to anyone I please. If you, then, will worship me, it will all be yours" (6:4). Jesus replied, "It is written, 'Worship the LORD your God, and serve only him.'" Worship implies following God's ways and plans rather than the devil's way of power, authority, and glory.

After the temptations, Luke writes, "When the devil had finished every test, he departed from him until an opportune time" (4:13). This does not mean that the devil took a rest or vacation. More than any other Gospel, Luke has demons or evil powers at work on almost every page. However, the "opportune time" refers to the direct conflict or temptations of Jesus that will begin at the time of his passion. This comes just before the Passover when the rulers were planning to put Jesus to death. "Then Satan entered into Judas called Iscariot, who was one of the twelve; he went away and conferred with the chief priests and officers of the temple police about how he might betray him to them" (22:3-4). Since the latter group cooperates with Judas, Luke sees them all together as the instruments of Satan in the coming narrative.

Despite this, Jesus treats Judas with special kindness at the Last Supper that follows. In contrast to Matthew he does not identify Judas before the supper, nor does Jesus say as in both Matthew and Mark that it would have been better if he had not been born. Only after the eucharistic words Jesus declares, "See, the one who betrays me is with me, and his hand is on the table. For the Son of Man is going as it has been determined, but woe to that one by whom he is betrayed" (22:21-22). Then they began to ask one another, which one of them could possibly do this. We will discuss in chapter 13 Jesus' Last Supper and Passover Meal.

The story of Jesus' agony in the garden and arrest contains a dramatic conflict between Jesus and Satan working in Judas and in his cohorts. We have already seen the essential elements in chapter 2 that establish Jesus as Messiah of peace and nonviolence. Here we can add a few details and outline the rest. Judas and his armed cohort came to arrest Jesus in the garden. Judas approached Jesus to kiss and identify him, but Jesus gave him a final chance to realize what he is about to do by telling him, "Judas, is it with a kiss that you are betraying the Son of Man?" (22:48).

Only Luke does not have Jesus' arrest immediately following. Instead, those with him, seeing what is about to happen, ask Jesus' permission to resist by striking out with their swords. However, they go ahead without waiting for Jesus' answer. The first casualty is the sliced ear of the high priest's servant. Jesus immediately calls for the fighting to stop and then heals the servant's ear. This is a reply to violence by love and healing. He then tells the crowd that he is not a violent leader, but one who teaches openly and peacefully each day in the Temple. Only Luke has his last words at the arrest, "This is your hour and the power of darkness" (22:53). What has happened is typical of the devil's workings by trusting in violence and power.

THE LAST TEMPTATIONS OF CHRIST ON THE CROSS
AND THE REOPENING OF PARADISE

In chapter 2 we saw the response of Jesus to his trial before the Sanhedrin and Pontius Pilate. Jesus defended himself as a Messiah of Peace. On the cross, we find the last onslaught of the devil in three final temptations of Jesus. First, the rulers scoffed at him saying, "He saved others; let him save himself if he is the Messiah of God, his chosen one!" (23:35). Second, the soldiers also mocked him, saying, "If you are the king of the Jews, save yourself!" Third, even one of the other crucified men derided him by declaring, "Are you not the Messiah? Save yourself and us!" Common to all three is questioning whether Jesus is really a messiah or king, someone who should have the power to save himself and others. Instead he seems completely helpless, weak, and disgraced, unable to save himself, let alone others.

However, the other crucified criminal declared that he was being punished justly for what he had done, while Jesus had done no wrong. So he said to Jesus, "Jesus, remember me when you come into your kingdom" (23:42). Jesus replied, "Truly I tell you, today you will be with me in Paradise." Despite his acute sufferings, these are Jesus' last words granting a crucified "terrorist" forgiveness and the privilege to be with him that very day in Paradise. "Paradise," translation of the Hebrew *Eden,* is where the devil's temptation prompted the sin of Adam and Eve and the closure of the gates of Paradise. Now they are reopened. Luke signals this victory over Satan by great cosmic signs, in the heavens as well as on earth: "It was now about noon, and darkness came over the whole land until three in the afternoon, while the sun's light failed; and the curtain of the temple was torn in two" (23:44-45).

Jesus' work on earth is now completed, so he places his own life and work in the hands of his Father in a final prayer: "Father, into your hands I commend my spirit." These hands are good indeed! The women who come to the tomb on the third day find it empty. Two dazzling bright angels announce to them, "Why do you look for the living among the dead? He is not here but risen" (24:5). The closing of the gates of Paradise for Adam and Eve had signaled death, but now new life has returned. This will be manifested by the activity of the presence and Spirit of Jesus in his disciples. Thus Peter will say to the crowds on Pentecost Day, "This Jesus God raised up, and of that all of us are witnesses. Being therefore exalted at the right hand of God, and having received from the Father the promise of the Holy Spirit, he has poured out this that you both see and hear" (2:32-33).

SUMMARY

The Sermon on the Plain proclaimed a new way to respond to evil and violence—active good toward the people behind it. Luke puts this in practice in the way he writes his Gospel. He sharply lessens threats such as hell, fire, Gehenna, or judgment. Jesus rebukes in proxy the prophet Elijah for his violent ways. Luke even edits the parables and stories in his tradition to eliminate unnecessary violence. Satan uses power and force through Judas and his cohorts at Jesus' arrest, but Jesus orders his disciples not to respond in violence. On the cross Jesus resists the last temptations of the devil and grants even a convicted repentant terrorist the privilege of being the first person to enter Paradise.

COROLLARY FOR TODAY

The growing crescendo of evil and violence in our world whether from individuals, groups, or nations is a constant temptation to forcibly put a stop to it by military means. Yet this drains us of the very resources we need to treat the roots of violence, which are often due to lack of justice to a large percentage of the world's population. In support of this, the following are statistics from the Center for Defense Information for the year 2002 in regard to military budget spending. The figures are only for those nations with major military capabilities. The United States leads the world with $343 billion dollars (projected to increase to around 365 billion for 2003, about a billion dollars a day). Next are all the NATO allies with $147 billion. Among these are Britain, $34.5 billion; France, $27 billion; and Germany, $23.3 billion.

Other major nations are Russia, $56 billion; Japan, $45.6 billion; China, $39.5 billion; India, $15.9 billion; South Korea, $12.8 billion; Australia, $7.1 billion; Pakistan, $3.3 billion. So outside of the United States the total comes to $258 billion (adding other countries would make the total much larger). But even here we see that the United States figure of $343 billion *is larger than all the other major nations combined*. The resources of the world cannot go on being increasingly devoted to military endeavors. Violence only breeds violence through military competition and taking away money that could be used to save the lives of hundreds of millions of people acutely suffering from hunger, poverty, and injustice.

9

The Sign of Jonah, the Comic Prophet of *Metanoia*

LUKE GIVES SPECIAL ATTENTION TO THE SIGN OF JONAH AS CON-nected with *metanoia*. Jesus declares that this is the only sign he will give: "This generation is an evil generation; it asks for a sign, but no sign will be given to it except the sign of Jonah. For just as Jonah became a sign to the people of Nineveh, so the Son of Man will be to this generation" (11:29-30).

Jonah belongs to the literary form often called "comic litera-ture," but beneath the surface it has a very serious message. It de-scribes the way to treat the most brutal enemy the Israelites ever had, the Assyrian empire. The Assyrians dominated Israel's history for over two hundred years. They captured the northern king-dom of Israel in 734 B.C. and made it into one of their provinces. They brought so many exiles into harsh exile that these originally ten tribes became considered as the "lost tribes of Israel."

The prophet Nahum has blistering descriptions of Assyria. The following is an excerpt addressed to Nineveh, her capital: "Ah! City of bloodshed, utterly deceitful, full of booty—no end to the plunder! The crack of whip and rumble of wheel, gallop-ing horse and bounding chariot! Horsemen charging, flashing sword and glittering spear, piles of dead, heaps of corpses, dead bodies without end—they stumble over the bodies!" (3:1-3).

However, the present book of Jonah dates from around the fifth century B.C. or after. Babylon succeeded Assyria as the next Middle East empire. They destroyed the Temple in 587 B.C. and brought leaders and many people into exile. However, the Babylonians allowed many of them to return at a later date. These exiles came back with renewed spirit to rebuild the Temple and reestablish the Torah. Yet many people had an exclusive, narrow attitude toward outsiders. The book of Jonah was written to counteract this spirit, using the example of Israel's former traditional enemy, the Assyrians. This was done in a humorous, gentle way to move readers to renounce stereotyped, narrow views of God and break the walls of separation between "enemies"—people of diverse ethnic and religious cultures. The book opens in this way:

> Now the word of the LORD came to Jonah son of Amittai, saying, "Go at once to Nineveh, that great city, and cry out against it; for their wickedness has come up before me." But Jonah set out to flee to Tarshish from the presence of the LORD. He went down to Joppa and found a ship going to Tarshish; so he paid his fare and went on board, to go with them to Tarshish, away from the presence of the LORD (1:1-3).

Right from this first verse we have strange paradoxes. God has never called upon a prophet to preach to any nation but Israel. Hebrew prophets preached to their own people, usually to give them hope against threats from other nations and to promise victory over them. So Jonah is thoroughly shocked. For him the call is so ridiculous that he immediately tries to flee in the opposite direction by taking a ship to Tarshish, a port in Spain, which was regarded in ancient times as the very end of the world.

Jonah is so provincial and narrow that he thinks God is only the God of the Hebrew land and that he can leave God's presence by taking a ship to Spain. But God shows that he is a God of all nature and determined in his desire to reach other people. He sends a mighty storm that threatens to destroy the little ship. The mariners then began to pray to their gods while Jonah, undisturbed, went down into the hold and fell fast asleep. This is a first lesson of the book—that so-called "pagans" can be more religious and prayerful than Jonah. The captain even came down to the hold to ask Jonah to pray to his God.

As the storm continued, the sailors cast lots to try to find out if someone's sin might be causing it. The lot fell on Jonah so they questioned him about his identity and origin. He replied, "I am a Hebrew, I worship the LORD, the God of heaven, who made the sea and the dry land" (1:9). This was really a confession of the universal nature of YHWH as a God of all of nature. Yet Jonah was not acting accordingly. The sailors then asked him what they should do to calm the sea in view of his guilt. Jonah replied that he should be thrown into the sea. However, the mariners were reluctant to do so and made every effort to reach land, but the sea only became stormier. Here we see that these foreigners had more sensitivity and respect for life than Jonah although respect for life was a primary biblical virtue.

In desperation, the sailors prayed to the LORD and asked that they not be held accountable for what they were forced to do. Then they threw Jonah into the sea which immediately became calm. The sailors then made a sacrifice to the LORD and offered prayers and vows. The prayers and sacrifices showed they now believed in the LORD and this tells readers that even strangers are capable of this faith. As for Jonah, "the LORD sent a large fish to swallow up Jonah and Jonah was in the belly of the fish three days and three nights" (1:17).

This symbolized an interior death experience for Jonah. He prayed to God and thanked him for his deliverance from death. However, his attitude to "his enemies" was not fundamentally changed. To Jonah's surprise these "enemies" of God later repented for what they had done. After three days the "whale" threw up Jonah on the shore. There God called Jonah a second time, saying, "Get up, go to Nineveh, that great city and proclaim to it the message that I tell you." This was, "Forty days more, and Nineveh shall be overthrown" (3:4). The word "overthrown" could have a double meaning either of being destroyed or turned over.

Jonah then began to walk across the city preaching his message. The author describes Nineveh as "exceedingly large" requiring three days to walk across. This is part of the great humorous exaggerations. Nineveh was indeed an enormous ancient city with walls seven and a half miles long, but nowhere near the size indicated in the book. At the close of Jonah, the writer notes there were a hundred thousand who could not tell their right hand from their left. Presumably these are the infants of a city much larger than the ancient ruins indicate. The comic elements include the animals not eating or drinking in repentance and even wearing sackcloth garments! (3:7-8; 4:11).

To Jonah's astonishment, "the people of Nineveh believed God; proclaimed a fast, and everyone, great and small put on sackcloth" (3:5). Everyone from the king down kept this fast, prayed to God, and turned from their evil ways and "the violence that was in their hands." This violence had been a characteristic of the ruthless Assyrian army. As a result, "When God saw what they did, how they turned from their evil ways, God changed his mind about the calamity that he had said he would bring upon them; and he did not do it" (3:10). When Jonah saw this he was furious because God had changed his mind about destroying Nineveh. He prayed to God in these words:

> O LORD! Is not this what I said while I was still in my own country? That is why I fled to Tarshish at the beginning; for I knew that you are a gracious God and merciful, slow to anger, and abounding in steadfast love, and ready to relent from punishing. And now, O LORD, please take my life from me, for it is better for me to die than to live (4:2-3).

This description of God comes from the three essential attributes of God that were revealed to Moses when God passed by, pronouncing his name YHWH, LORD (Exod 34:6-7). These are "gracious," *chanun*, "merciful," *rachum*, womb-compassionate; and "steadfast love," *chesed*, mindful of covenants. They describe a God of complete impartial justice, loving all people of every race, every belief, and even enemies of Israel. This is simply too much for Jonah who wanted to quit life right at this point. He does not want to live in a world not governed by the laws of "justice" in which he grew up. But God loves Jonah, his stubborn reactionary, and has a lesson for him too. The Lord said to him, "Is it right for you to be angry?"

Meanwhile, Jonah built himself a shelter from the hot sun out of a bush near the city and sat down to watch what would happen to the city. He was still waiting for it to be struck by God, perhaps by an earthquake, in punishment for its sins. On the next day, however, he found that the bush had dried up and he was in danger of being scorched by the blazing sun. Once again he asked that he might die. God said to him, "Are you angry about the bush?" He replied, "Yes, angry enough to die." God's response, the last line of the book, needs no further comment than the words themselves:

> Then the LORD said, "You are concerned about the bush, for which you did not labor and which you did not grow; it came into being in a night and perished in a night. And should I not be concerned about Nineveh, that great city, in which there are more than a hundred and twenty thousand persons who do not know their right hand from their left, and also many animals?" (4:10-11).

SUMMARY

The book of Jonah shows that God's love and mercy is open to all people without distinction, even those who have proven to be the worst enemies. The book says nothing about distinctions between various religions or denominations. The God of all humans, nature, animals, plants, and living beings is accessible to all. His highest attributes of mercy, grace, and steadfast love are likewise for all. Jonah in this book exemplifies a prophetic vocation to go out to any individual or nation, even those ordinarily considered enemies. A friend of God can never remain an enemy to Jonah or anyone else.

COROLLARY FOR TODAY

Although the name of Jonah may be accidental, no Hebrew Bible reader could ever forget that it has the meaning of "dove." The dove is the messenger of peace and harmony that notifies Noah that the chaotic deluge has come to a close. The dove is a favorite title for a lover in the Song of Songs, occurring six times. It is a symbol of God's people Israel. At the baptism of Jesus the dove appears over Jesus' head and God's voice pronounced him to be his beloved son. The prophet Jonah at first felt that his mission was to be more like a hawk to punish God's enemies and his own. The book calls us to a ministry of peace and reconciliation based on the inner meaning of God, his *rachum*, inner compassion for all. No one can really be an enemy who has been made to God's image and created with the inner capability to be God's friend.

10

Women of Peace and Courage

WOMEN'S ROLES IN THE PROCESS OF PEACE

IN CHAPTER 5, WE SAW HOW LUKE BROUGHT TOGETHER FORGIVE-ness and *metanoia*. This was to show that reconciliation and peace include the healing of relationships. In this whole process, initiative, invitation, favor, or grace plays a central role. This "grace" is from the Hebrew root verb *chanan* or the noun *chan-nun*. This is one of the three great attributes of God revealed to Moses, his "womb-compassion," *rachum*, his "covenant love," *chesed*, and his "graciousness," *channun*, when Moses asked to see God's face (Exod 34:6). The Greek Old Testament often trans-lates this last as *charis*. Peace means wholeness so it must include *charis* in God as well as in people.

In Luke, women will be prominent in showing *charis* by tak-ing the initiative to move toward the fullness of peace. This means they will also be women of courage for it takes daring and risk to take that first step, often in the face of opposition. *Charis* is a specialty word in Luke among the Gospels, occurring nine times. In Luke's Acts of the Apostles it is found sixteen times. The verb *charizomai*, "to graciously give," is only in Luke. In ad-dition, the verb *charitoō*, "to be specially favored," occurs once in Luke only. This is in the angel Gabriel's greeting to Mary

(1:28) and in the letter to the Ephesians (1:6). While these words will not always be used about women, they capture the special characteristic behind many important women's roles.

GOD'S SCRIPTURAL PLAN FOR WOMEN'S EQUAL PLACE IN THE MESSIANIC ERA

A second area of concern for Luke will be fulfillment of Scripture, as he indicated in the first verse of his Gospel. He declares that he intends to provide "an orderly account of the events that have been fulfilled among us." In correspondence, in Luke's second volume, Acts, Peter's first words after Pentecost are a scriptural quotation of the prophet Joel:

> Then afterward I will pour out my spirit on all flesh; your sons and your daughters shall prophesy, your old men shall dream dreams, and your young men shall see visions. Even on the male and female slaves, in those days, I will pour out my spirit (Joel 2:28-29; Acts 2:17-18).

In the above verses we find a repeated emphasis on the equal working of the Spirit in both men and women. Luke feels that this is a supreme sign of the Spirit, central to the universal theme of his Gospel. The conclusion of Joel's prophecy states, "Then everyone who calls on the name of the LORD will be saved" (Acts 2:21). This explains Luke's concern for the leadership of women in the rest of Acts of the Apostles. Even before Pentecost, Luke was careful to note the prominent place of women in the assembly: First, he names all the apostles by name and then writes: "All these were constantly devoting themselves to prayer, together with certain women, including Mary the mother of Jesus, as well as his brothers" (1:14). We will later outline the central role of women in *Acts*, but first we will study their place in Luke's Gospel.

ELIZABETH, "FIRST LADY" OF THE NEW TESTAMENT

Luke first distinguishes her by her lineage. Not only is she a direct descendent of Aaron, the first Levite priest, but she also bears the same name as Aaron's wife. This paves the way for the extraordinary role that she will play as the spark that starts the new messianic era. In chapter 3 we described the surprising events leading to the birth of the Baptist. When Zechariah came out of the Temple unable to speak or pronounce the priestly blessing of peace, he must have soon indicated to his wife by gesture or writing what had happened. Knowing his doubts and hesitation, Elizabeth knew she must take a special initiative. The angel had told Zechariah that she would bear a son and that John would be his name (1:13).

More than anyone else, Elizabeth knew the obstacles in the way. She was getting on in years and hopes of childbearing were slim as well as fraught with danger. If a child were born, how long would she be able to nourish and care for him in preparation for his extraordinary ministry? Also, the story begins with the ominous mention of King Herod, who would certainly try to imprison and execute anyone connected with messianic expectations. Would she be raising a child destined for a cruel death? Her fears were realized when a later Herod actually beheaded the Baptist as a young man (3:19-20; 9:7-9), but she probably had already died by that time.

The name "John" must have affected her decision to go ahead. In Hebrew it was *yehochanan* meaning "God is gracious." The first letters *(yeho)* are an abbreviation of YHWH and the last ones, *chanan*, "gracious," are the great quality of God as grace that we saw in the revelation of God's name to Moses. The words announce the theme of grace in Luke and were a signal to Elizabeth to begin the initiative that the name John implied. The decisive time for her to act arrived during the circumcision rite for her child, eight days after birth. The patriarchal family heads had already decided to name the child after Zechariah his father and were preparing to do so. But Elizabeth courageously opposed the predominant male enclave and declared, "No; he is to be called John" (1:60). So thinking that she would not oppose her husband, the group asked Zechariah to choose the child's name. To their surprise, he gestured for a tablet and wrote, "His name is John."

All the people were amazed. At this point, Zechariah's tongue was loosened and he began to speak, blessing and praising God.

MARY, THE *KECHARITŌMENĒ*

The mother of Jesus is the only person in the Bible who ever received this title, often translated "favored one" from the rare verb we saw above, *charitoō* from the root *charis*. Thus she is the exemplar of divine initiative in the Gospels. The angel does not greet her with the common Aramaic "peace be with you," but with a Greek greeting, *kaire*, literally "rejoice," followed by "favored one." This greeting brings out the roots of the peace greeting. Mary is perplexed by this greeting (1:29), so the angel assures her that it is for her by saying, "Do not be afraid, *Mary*, for you have found favor, *charis* with God." Even more than Elizabeth, a conception announcement is a shocking challenge to a young lady, recently affianced to Joseph. She answers, "How can this be, since I am a virgin?" (1:34). The angel assures her the child will be from the Holy Spirit and that even her aged cousin Elizabeth shall bear a child, for "nothing will be impossible with God." Then Mary answered with courage, "Here am I, the servant of the Lord; let it be with me according to your word" (1:37).

The reception of God's *charis* prompts Mary in turn to show the same *charis* to others. Once she had learned about her cousin Elizabeth, Mary went quickly on the difficult journey from Nazareth to the Judean hill country. She stayed with her aged cousin three months to help her until the birth of her child. Luke relates that when she arrived

> She entered the house of Zechariah and *greeted* Elizabeth. When Elizabeth heard Mary's *greeting*, the child leaped in her womb. And Elizabeth was filled with the Holy Spirit and exclaimed with a loud cry, "Blessed are you among women, and blessed is the fruit of your womb. And why has this happened to me, that the mother of my Lord comes to me? For as soon as I heard the sound of your *greeting*, the child in my womb leaped

for joy. And blessed is she who believed that there would be a fulfillment of what was spoken to her by the Lord" (1:41-45).

The word "greeting" is italicized to show its triple repetition. This would have consisted in the ordinary greeting, followed by a kiss and embrace of peace. For Luke and the ancient world, the greeting of a holy person or messenger carried with it a special inner *dynamis*. This is illustrated in Jesus' instructions to the seventy missionaries: "Whatever house you enter, first say, 'Peace to this house!' And if anyone is there who shares in peace, your peace will rest on that person; but if not, it will return to you" (10:5). In the story above, Mary becomes the exemplar of those who take the initiative to reach out and greet those who need their support and presence. In doing so, they carry like Mary, the Spirit within them to others.

THE PERPETUALLY CONTAGIOUS
AND "UNCLEAN" WOMAN

As he (Jesus) went, the crowds pressed in on him. Now there was a woman who had been suffering from hemorrhages for twelve years; and though she had spent all she had on physicians, no one could cure her. She came up behind him and touched the fringe of his clothes, and immediately her hemorrhage stopped. Then Jesus asked, "Who touched me?" When all denied it, Peter said, "Master, the crowds surround you and press in on you." But Jesus said, "Someone touched me; for I noticed that power had gone out from me" (8:42-46).

This woman suffered from an abnormal menstrual flow. Because of the taboos on menstrual blood in Leviticus 15:19-30, she was continually ritually unclean. In addition, the laws declared that this was so contagious that anyone either touching her, her clothing, or her furniture would become unclean also. This meant that she was virtually a social outcast. She had no hopes for marriage or children. In fact she could not even greet anyone, for that implied an embrace and kiss. Anyone who did

touch her or her things, even accidentally, would become unclean also until evening and be required to bathe and even wash
their clothes.

For her to dare approach and touch Jesus' clothes (regarded
as his person) amounted to an act of heroic courage. She risked
disgrace, public humiliation, and severe punishment. Yet she
trusted in a cure as well as acceptance and sneaked up behind
Jesus to touch the corner of his cloak. On doing so, she immediately sensed within that she was cured. At the same time Jesus
also sensed from within, literally, that a flow of *dynamis* had
gone out from him to her. He immediately asked, "Who touched
me?" Everyone denied it because the woman's actions had been
so secretive.

> When the woman saw that she could not remain hidden, she
> came trembling; and falling down before him, she declared in
> the presence of all the people why she had touched him, and
> how she had been immediately healed. He said to her, "Daugh-
> ter, your faith has made you well; go in peace" (8:47-48).

Jesus' final greeting of peace was a moment not to be forgotten in a lifetime. No one had dared to greet or embrace her for
twelve whole years. She had once again received wholeness or
peace within herself, and now she could give it to others in the
restoration of relationships. Jesus also gave the same final greeting to the forgiven woman in Luke 7:50, which we have seen in
chapter 5. He said to her, "Daughter, your faith has made you
well; go in peace" (8:49). In doing so, Jesus gave her the greeting
no one else had been able to give her for twelve years. This is because it would have required touching her in embrace and thus
acquiring her uncleanness.

WOMEN AND THE MYSTERY OF THE CROSS:
THE FIRST TO REMEMBER

Courage, risk, and daring are at the heart of the mystery of
the cross where women play an essential role. In Matthew and

Mark, women seem "nowhere" yet are really "everywhere" as we find their names and witness at the three essential events: the death, burial, and resurrection of Jesus. Yet those Gospels indicate that the women had followed Jesus and accompanied him all the way from Galilee to Jerusalem. This shows that they were present in all the great events that previously took place. However, Luke wants to make this much clearer by naming them earlier in his Gospel—before the sending of the Twelve (9:1).

> Soon afterwards he went on through cities and villages, proclaiming and bringing the good news of the kingdom of God. The twelve were with him, as well as some women who had been cured of evil spirits and infirmities: Mary, called Magdalene, from whom seven demons had gone out, and Joanna, the wife of Herod's steward Chuza, and Susanna, and many others, who provided for them out of their resources (8:1-3).

Luke has a special motive for bringing in the women's names at this point. He wants to be sure the gospel listeners know that the women actually hear Jesus' words in the three predictions about his coming death and suffering (9:21-22, 44-45; 18:31-34). The predictions are progressive, revealing more and more. The following is the last as Jesus declared:

> See, we are going up to Jerusalem, and everything that is written about the Son of Man by the prophets will be accomplished. For he will be handed over to the Gentiles; and he will be mocked and insulted and spat upon. After they have flogged him, they will kill him, and on the third day he will rise again. But they understood nothing about all these things; in fact, what he said was hidden from them, and they did not grasp what was said (18:31-34).

In the above verses we find the essential points that Jesus' suffering and death will not be a terrible misfortune, but part of a plan of God in the Scriptures. This plan comes from the mind of God and cannot be possibly fathomed by any human being. So it is hidden from them at present. The particular Scripture mentioned is that of the "Son of Man." This Son of Man scripture is found while describing the most disgraceful and humiliating event in the history of Israel. This was the closing and defilement of the holy Temple by Greek rulers between 167–164 B.C. The reopening and rededication of the Temple in triumph was celebrated by Jesus and continues to be celebrated by the Jewish people in the feast of *channukah,* meaning rededication.

In Daniel's prophecy he has a vision of God as "the Ancient One" seated on his throne and convening the divine court in judgment. Daniel writes, "I saw one like a human being (literally "Son of Man") coming with the clouds of heaven. He came to the Ancient One and was presented before him. To him was given dominion and glory and kingship, that all peoples, nations, and languages should serve him. His dominion is an everlasting dominion that shall not pass away, and his kingship is one that shall never be destroyed" (7:13-14).

Following this, Daniel applies this prophecy to Israel which is represented by the corporate figure "Son of Man." The nation has been utterly disgraced and humiliated but God will intervene and raise her up to establish an everlasting kingdom. In this reversal God has transformed the worst in human weakness and disgrace by making it into a surprising triumph when the Temple was reopened. For this reason, the Son of Man scriptures will be an important basis for understanding the cross in the Gospel.

We can now comprehend the central scene of Luke as he describes the women coming to the empty tomb and meeting angels who announce to them, "Why do you look for the living among the dead? He is not here, but has risen. *Remember* how he told you, while he was still in Galilee, that the Son of Man must be handed over to sinners, and be crucified, and on the third day rise again" (24:5-7). The climactic words then follow: *"Then they remembered his words."* The women then returned from the tomb and told this to the eleven and the rest. The specific names of the women follow: "Now it was Mary Magdalene, Joanna, Mary the mother of James, and the other women with them who told this to the apostles" (24:10).

All this has tremendous consequences. These women are the first to remember and make possible the continuity of Jesus' mission to the world. Without them, the history of Jesus would have ended at this point. *Remembrance*, for Luke, is the key to the future. He will stress this in his description of Jesus' Last Supper and Passover meal, which we will study in chapter 13. This remembrance only came about because these woman had the daring initiative and courage to stand by Jesus even at the cross. Especially at Passover time, the soldiers would have been very concerned to look for friends and supporters of those whom they crucified. Luke has prepared from the beginning this theme of remembrance. He notes twice how Mary treasured in her heart the words and events concerning Jesus' birth and childhood (1:19; 2:51). This treasuring or pondering would have included reflection on the Scriptures. The foreshadowing of Jesus' suffering and death certainly came from Simeon's words to her: "This child is destined for the falling and the rising of many in Israel, and to be a sign that will be opposed so that the inner thoughts of many will be revealed—and a sword will pierce your own soul too" (2:34-35).

WOMEN'S FOUNDATIONAL ROLE
IN THE ACTS OF THE APOSTLES

After Jesus' death, the beginning of Jesus' Church was fraught with many difficulties and even persecution from Jewish and Roman authorities. So the initiative of women in the formative stages of Christian communities was essential. Among these initiatives, we note the following: Luke notes that the mother of Jesus and a group of women were present in the first assembly of 120 that prayed and waited for the coming of the Spirit on the first Pentecost. Meetings of the Jerusalem church took place at the household of a woman called Mary, the mother of John/Mark (12:12). This young man accompanied Paul and Barnabas on their first apostolic journey (13:5).

The entry of the Gospel into Europe was a great important turning point in the early Church. When Paul first came to

Philippi, he found that a group of women had gathered outside the city gate to pray by a river. One of them was a lady from Thyatira called Lydia, who was a prominent business woman in the purple cloth industry. She became a convert of Paul and welcomed him into her own household, where all became baptized. Lydia's household became Paul's first church in Europe. In turn, the community became Paul's favorite church that followed him with letters and funds to allow him to preach the Gospel more freely (Phil 4:15-17).

A married couple, Aquila and Priscilla, were Christians who came to Corinth from Rome since the Emperor Claudius had expelled all Jews from Rome (Acts 18:2). They were tent-makers like Paul and invited him to stay at their house, which became a Christian meeting place. Priscilla seems to have been the more active apostle than Aquila since Luke twice mentions her first (18:18, 26). The dedicated couple made an important breakthrough in converting Apollos, a noted preacher and disciple of John the Baptist (18:24-26). Apollos later became an important Christian leader in Corinth (1 Cor 1:12; 3:4-6, 22; 4:6; 16:12).

Paul had such confidence in the couple, especially Priscilla, that he sent them on ahead to make new beginnings in Ephesus, capital of the Roman province of Asia and one of the largest cities in the empire. At the end of his letter to the Romans, Paul sent a very special greeting to them: "Greet Prisca and Aquila, who work with me in Christ Jesus, and who risked their necks for my life, to whom not only I give thanks, but also all the churches of the Gentiles" (16:3). Luke also pays tribute to younger unmarried women. In Paul's final journey to Jerusalem, he stayed at the house of the evangelist Philip. He had four unmarried daughters who had the gift of prophecy (21:10). The Acts of the Apostles also pays tribute to a woman called Dorcas who was part of a widow's community where she distinguished herself for her works of charity. When she died, the community sent for Peter who came and raised her from the dead (9:32-42).

THE HOUSEHOLD AND
THE NEW RELIGIOUS ROLE OF WOMEN

In the Old Testament, we have followed the original Hebrew in referring to God as "He." We have not done so to bring out a gender characteristic of God. The actual Hebrew word for God is *Elohim*, which is a masculine form. Why is it so? Because the Old Testament describes a family covenant that God makes with his people. Such a covenant is only made by the father as head of the family or household. Due to the whole patriarchal structure of the Old Testament, this was always a man, with very rare exceptions in case of widows or prostitutes. God could not be described as a family head unless in those terms. The firstborn son succeeded the father in this role.

In the ancient Hebrew world, the father was not only the financial head of the household, but the priest as well. Later, Moses substituted his own tribe of Levi to replace the traditional priestly role of the firstborn son. However, as a relic of the ancient custom, every firstborn son had to be offered to God in this role and then bought back. So we see that after the birth of Jesus his parents brought him to Jerusalem to present him to the Lord (Luke 2:22).

However, after the Gospel moved into the Greek world, we find that Luke makes specific mention of women as heads of the household, like Lydia in Philippi, whom we have previously described. Her household followed Lydia in her baptism. As household head, Lydia would have led worship services and liturgy. The same was probably true in the "house" of a certain Mary in Acts 12:12. Likewise, of Nympha, whom Paul salutes in the letter to the Colossians along with "the church in *her* house" (4:5). Centuries have now passed since men only were considered to be "heads of household." This is a fact well recognized even by Internal Revenue tax forms!

SUMMARY

In concern for fulfillment of Scripture, Luke highlights Joel's prophecy about the final messianic era and the equal sharing of the Spirit regardless of gender differences. In this matter women have special roles in the process of peace. *Charis*, "favor," "grace," or "initiative," is a feature of Luke and especially manifest in the women of this Gospel, like Elizabeth and Mary. In the mystery of the cross and resurrection, it is the women who heard his words and were the first to remember them at the empty tomb. In the Acts of the Apostles, women hold important leadership roles in the Jerusalem church. Women like Lydia and Priscilla had foundational roles in bringing the Gospel to new areas like Europe and the Roman province of Asia. Women as heads of family, like Lydia, not only supervised household finances but also led these extended households in prayer and liturgy.

COROLLARY FOR TODAY

The sparkling enthusiasm and initiative of women played an essential part in the foundation and growth of the early Church. In Luke's Greek world, they had primary leadership positions in the extended family and business households that were usually held by men. As such they would be in charge and *preside not only in business matters but in worship and liturgy as well.* The prophecy of Joel tells us that the messianic age cannot really come about without full equality for women not only in society but in the churches also. Each step and courageous stand to make that a reality brings out a new freshness and renewal of the Church that is not only indispensable for growth but will turn around disastrous declines that have come about because of the lack of women's leadership.

11

An Upside-down World: Peace and the Priority of Little Ones

IN CHAPTER 1, LUKE DESCRIBED JESUS' BIRTH AS INWARDLY SUBVERSIVE to the outer force and power of the Roman Empire. Hence it was "turning the world upside-down" (Acts 17:6). Luke returns to this theme in his great journey to Jerusalem section (9:51–19:27). This section contains most of Luke's special stories and parables. His aim is to present this journey as a Christian "Way" of peace for the gospel audience. The "Way" (odos) is a favorite name for early believers found nineteen times in the Acts of the Apostles. This "Way" will be largely based on the spirit of "little ones" so it will have a literary frame of two children's stories around it as an introduction and conclusion of this theme. After Jesus makes his third announcement that he is going to Jerusalem to suffer, we find the introductory preparation for the journey:

> An argument arose among them as to which one of them was the greatest. But Jesus, aware of their inner thoughts, took a little child and put it by his side, and said to them, "Whoever welcomes this child in my name welcomes me, and whoever welcomes me welcomes the one who sent me; for the least among all of you is the greatest" (9:46-48).

Jesus is aware of what lies beneath the above argument among his disciples. It is competition for places of authority and power if he establishes himself in Jerusalem, the capital. Jesus teaches by a striking visible contrast in bringing the most power-less person to his side (a position of power). He identifies to such an extent with the child that to receive a child is to receive him-self and God who sent him. Then Jesus declares that the least, *mikroteros*, among them will be the greatest, *megas*. This sets the tone for Jesus' journey and the way for believers. A little one, *mikros*, or child will be the model. These little ones will not only be actual children but will include all those at society's lowest rungs, for example outsiders and those looked down upon as fringe elements. The closing of the literary frame will be another story of children in 18:15-17.

A brief example of these "outsiders" follows. There was an exorcist outside of Jesus' circle who was casting out devils in his name. The disciples tried to stop him from doing so, but Jesus said, "Do not stop him; for whoever is not against you is for you" (9:49-50). This story may be modeled on Moses' experience when God granted him seventy assistants and poured the spirit upon them. There were two others not present at the time who also received the spirit and were acting accordingly. Joshua, the assistant of Moses said to him, "My lord, stop them!" But Moses said to him, "Are you jealous for my sake? Would that all the LORD's people were prophets, and that the LORD would put his spirit on them!" (Num 11:29). In these accounts we find the same spirit of jealousy and competition that Jesus contrasts with the spirit of a child.

THE BEGINNING OF THE JOURNEY
AND THE REFUSAL OF HOSPITALITY TO JESUS

"When the days drew near for him to be taken up, he set his face to go to Jerusalem. And he sent messengers ahead of him." On their way they entered a village of the Samaritans to make ready for him; but they did not receive him, because his face was set toward Jerusalem (9:51-53). The Samaritans were traditional enemies, regarded as outsiders. This was especially true when travelers came through on the way to Jerusalem, where Samaritans were excluded from the Temple. Jesus' disciples James and John were outraged at their refusal of hospitality and asked Jesus if they could use power to call down lightning from the sky to punish them. Here again the disciples showed their attraction to power and force. Jesus, however rebuked them and they went to another village for lodging. In the journey that follows, Jesus will turn values upside-down and reply to "enemy" Samaritans by granting them a special role in parable and story.

THE SPIRIT OF FELLOW TRAVELERS WITH JESUS

"As they were going along the road, someone said to him, 'I will follow you wherever you go'" (9:57). This mention of a road, or way, is one of several travel links in the journey section. The main question in 9:57-62 is the relationship to traditional patriarchal authority in society. Here Jesus overturns this again by saying that while foxes and birds have nests the Son of Man has nowhere to lay his head. Leaving the security of parental resources may mean the threat of homelessness.

A second question of returning to bury one's father is not a matter of actually going to a burial, which would be an obligation as in the case of the burial of John the Baptist (Mark 6:29). It was a society custom to stay close to the parental household until their death. That is why Jesus brings out the priority of the kingdom, "Let the dead bury their own dead; but as for you, go and proclaim the kingdom of God" (9:60). So a child is first of all a child of a heavenly Father.

The next episode of the appointment of seventy other disciples really follows from this. The number seventy represents the spreading of the Gospel to the world. Traditionally, seventy as a full number represented all the nations. Without the emotional and financial support of traditional religious or parental authority, "fellow travelers" will have to trust that they have been *sent* by Jesus or the Lord of the harvest (10:1-2). Again a third and fourth time, "*Go* on your way. See, *I am sending you*" (10:3).

Since disciples have been sent by God, they can trust that there will be people who will offer them hospitality, so there is no need to carry food, extra money, and clothes (10:4). When they enter a house, they will greet it with the words, "Peace to this house." Their greeting, as people sent by God, will have the power of God's own greeting and will bring peace if people are open to it (10:5). Those who are not receptive will be responsible to God. The identification with Jesus, as children (9:48) is repeated as Jesus says, "Whoever listens to you listens to me" (10:16).

The connection to children continues as Jesus rejoices in the Holy Spirit when the seventy return in success. He prays, "I thank you, Father, Lord of heaven and earth, because you have hidden these things from the wise and the intelligent and have revealed them to infants; yes, Father, for such was your gracious will" (10:21). Jesus' instructions to the seventy were really foolish and impossible from a worldly, "prudent" viewpoint. Only a child or "infant" would believe and follow them. However a true "child" would take seriously Jesus' triple word that they were *sent* with all the divine power and that "nothing will be impossible with God." These last words were addressed to Mary by the angel Gabriel (1:37).

AN ENEMY AND OUTSIDER
BECOMES THE BEST TEACHER

Among the "little ones" of the journey are outsiders like the Samaritan in the next story (10:29-37). Here again we find a great reversal. In the religious establishment the Levite and the priest held the highest rank as closest to God in their service of the Temple. Yet in this story both men passed by a wounded man lying at the edge of the road. It is not that the Levite and priest were bad people. They were "extremely" good, anxious to keep all the laws of legal purity surrounding their office. The wounded man looked like he was dead and to touch him would make them unclean and unable to perform their priestly duties.

On the other hand the Samaritan was the typical "bad person." They refused to have any part with the Temple that meant so much to the priests and people. They did not even offer Jesus and his disciples hospitality as he passed through Samaria. The Samaritan was oblivious of all the legalities that made the priest and Levite steer clear on the other side of the road. However, as a little one and child, he drew near to the wounded man and was deeply moved with compassion, *esplangchnisthē*. Then the Samaritan responded to the needs of the man in a total, extraordinary way. In doing so, he was acting in accord with the highest ideal in the Sermon on the Plain, when Jesus declared, "Be merciful, even as your Father is merciful" (6:36).

We have seen in chapter 6, that "merciful" corresponds to being moved by the *splangchna* or inner compassion of God, corresponding to *rachum*, God's highest attribute of womb compassion. We can now understand why Luke has an introduction to this story in the lawyer's question as to which is the greatest commandment of the Law. Only Luke has Jesus' answer in the form of one unseparated command, not two (the *addition* of love of neighbor as in the other previous gospels). Jesus replies in the words of the daily *Shema*, "You shall love the Lord your God with all your heart and with all your soul, and with all your strength, and with all your mind *and your neighbor as yourself*" (10:27). The lawyer then asked, "And who is my neighbor?" These words introduce the Samaritan story. So at the end Jesus can ask the lawyer in turn who was the person who proved to be neighbor to the man mugged by robbers. The lawyer answered, "The one who showed him mercy." Jesus then concludes by saying to the lawyer and the gospel audience of any time, "Go and do likewise" (10:37).

THE SPIRIT OF A CHILD AND LITTLE ONE IN PRAYER

This spirit is that of praying to God as the kindest of parents who cannot refuse anything to a child. The model is that of the Lord's prayer in Luke, which we have seen in chapter 5. Children are known for their persistence that eventually "wears out" parents. So we have the humorous story only in Luke of a friend arriving at midnight to make the ridiculous request of bread for some guests who have just come to town. Only persistence finally rouses the whole household to prepare and bake bread (11:5-8). The persevering nature of "Ask and you shall receive" is often missed. It is a present Greek tense, equivalent to the English, "Keep on asking and you will receive." This is repeated in three images: asking, seeking and knocking. Then the whole message is repeated in an entirely different form, "For everyone who asks, receives, and everyone who searches finds, and for everyone who knocks it shall be opened" (11:10). The persistent atmosphere cannot be missed.

On the other side, God is not a reluctant parent, but one who would never betray a child's trust and wants to give the utmost to a beloved child: "Is there anyone among you who, if your child asks for a fish, will give a snake instead of a fish? Or if the child asks for an egg, will give a scorpion? If you then, who are evil, know how to give good gifts to your children, how much more will the heavenly Father give the Holy Spirit to those who ask him!" (11:11-13).

LITTLE ONES, ANIMALS AND ALL CREATION: FINDING HARMONY AND PEACE IN LIFE

Children are not the only ones that God cares for in an interconnected universe. The creator is concerned about animals, plants, and all creatures. Examples are given in 12:22-31: "Consider the ravens: they neither sow nor reap, they have neither storehouse nor barn, and yet God feeds them." "Consider the lilies, how they grow, even Solomon in all his glory was not clothed as one of these." Openness to all of creation and gratitude for God's gifts results in a positive and joyful attitude toward life. A reference to "Solomon in all his glory" (12:27) recalls the wisdom tradition. When God offered to give king Solomon him anything he wished, he only asked for (literally) a "listening heart" so he could make good decisions for his people

(1 Kgs 3:9). God was pleased with his request and granted him as a gift everything else besides.

In contrast, the great enemy is excessive worry whether for food, clothing, a long life, or money (as in the previous parable of the rich fool). All this leads to a continual "striving" or pre-occupation that consumes life itself. "For it is the nations of the world that strive after all these things and your heavenly Father knows that you need them." The only remedy is a trusting focus on God's gift of his kingdom: "Instead, strive for his kingdom and all these things will be given to you as well" (12:31).

LITTLE ONES BUT NOT "MARSHMALLOWS": OPPOSITION TO FALSE PROMISES OF PEACE

Jesus once declared, "Do you think that I have come to bring peace to the earth? No, I tell you, but rather division! From now on five in one household will be divided, three against two and two against three" (12:51-52). Jesus' words have sometimes been misunderstood because he uses the same words as the angel at his birth: "Peace on Earth." His message is not that of external complacency that avoids conflict, dissension, and disagreement. The Word of God in the prophets tended to polarize people one way or another to take definite stands. Likewise, followers of Jesus who stand up for their values of true peace resulting from nonviolent but positive action will meet with strong opposition, even within their households.

As a prophet, Jesus had to go to the capital city with his message about good news for the poor as a priority. Yet he knew this meant risking his life. He lamented, "Jerusalem, Jerusalem, the city that kills the prophets and stones those who are sent to it! How often have I desired to gather your children together as a hen gathers her brood under her wings, and you were not willing!" (13:34). The image of hen and chicks is a way to show that his approach was like that of a mother concerned for little ones yet willing to protect them with his life if necessary.

AN AXIOM AND TEST FOR LITTLE ONES: "THOSE WHO HUMBLE THEMSELVES WILL BE EXALTED"

Only Luke has this saying in two places (14:11 and 18:14). We have studied the first parable story in chapter 12. There, those who push themselves into first places in wedding banquets find themselves reversed into the last place by others and by God. Those "little ones" who humbly choose a low place find that God intervenes to raise them up. At the end we find Jesus saying, "Those who humble themselves will be exalted."

The second parable has a dramatic setting describing two men who went up to the Temple to pray, one a Pharisee, the other a tax collector. In Jesus' time and in that of Luke, a Pharisee was a person who embodied all that was holy through zeal for perfect observance of the Law, even in the most minute matters. As respected and popular teachers, they were the cream of Judaism. The Pharisee stood up confidently and prayed in this manner: "God, I thank you that I am not like other people: thieves, rogues, adulterers, or even like this tax collector. I fast twice a week; I give a tenth of all my income" (18:11-12). Actually what the Pharisee was doing was little short of heroic. The law of tithing involved oil, grain, and wine, but the Pharisee even gave one tenth of all his income (even garden herbs!) to the Temple. His fasting and prayer took in two whole days a week.

However, he judged others by comparison, which was opposed to the Sermon on the Plain where Jesus advised not to judge others, lest God judge us accordingly. In contrast, the view of other people should be that of God: "Be merciful, as your Father is merciful" (6:36). In addition, the Pharisee had "pushed his way" to righteousness by his own efforts to become "not like other people." The tax collector, however had no presumptions about who he was. He acknowledged he was a sinner, a betrayer of his own people through a livelihood by injustice and service of foreign Roman oppressors.

Jesus' description of the tax collector is simple but very moving: "But the tax collector, standing far off, would not even look up to heaven, but was beating his breast and saying, 'God, be merciful to me, a sinner!'" He does not push himself forward but stands at a distance and appeals to God's mercy. Jesus then declares that God exalts and grants him mercy as a gift: "I tell you, this man went down to his home justified rather than the other; for all who exalt themselves will be humbled, but all who humble themselves will be exalted" (18:14).

THE BLESSING OF CHILDREN AND
CLOSE OF THE LITERARY FRAME ON LITTLE ONES

> People were bringing even infants to him that he might touch them; and when the disciples saw it, they sternly ordered them not to do it. But Jesus called for them and said, "Let the little children come to me, and do not stop them; for it is to such as these that the kingdom of God belongs. Truly I tell you, whoever does not receive the kingdom of God as a little child will never enter it" (18:15-17).

This is the close of the literary frame on children and little ones that began with a similar story in 12:46-48. For dramatic contrast Jesus refers to "infants" and twice to little children. In both stories, there is a contrast to the disciples who either try to stop the children or argue about who is the greatest. The touching of the children is in the same sense as the *dynamis* of Jesus' touch often seen in Luke. Jesus is imparting his own presence and power as a gift. Every adult must then remain a child at heart in order to receive the kingdom as this gift.

SUMMARY

Luke has a "great journey" narrative in 9:51–19:27 that is introduced by a literary frame on children and little ones. During the journey these little ones are found in stories that include outsiders, the marginalized, and those on the lowest rungs of the society ladder. Jesus' upside-down theology is reflected in the proverb, "All who exalt themselves will be humbled, and those who humble themselves will be exalted." This means adopting the attitude of a child if one wishes to enter the kingdom of God.

COROLLARY FOR TODAY

Our modern technological world is distinguished by an ever growing complexity and effort to accomplish goals on a large scale through huge organizations and even globalization. However, acquiring the attitude of a child while remaining an adult cannot be accomplished by any kind of technology. It can only be reached by striving for simplicity in the use of material goods and by giving priority to personal relationships in the atmosphere of small groups. A small child can learn any language in the world perfectly, something beyond the reach of adults. That is because they hear without previous programming of what they should be hearing. "Becoming a child again" means recovering the ability to be really exposed, touched, moved, and changed by the universe around us, whether it is people, animals, plants, or nature.

This was the lesson of the Good Samaritan.

12

Bread and Circuses versus Jesus' New World Food Language

THE SIGN OF THE MANGER: NOURISHMENT FOR THE WORLD, NOT "BREAD AND CIRCUSES"

OCTAVIAN, THE FIRST CAESAR AUGUSTUS, USED THE TERM "BREAD and circuses" (found in the writing of the first-century poet Juvenal) to sum up the means to ensure peace and win the favor of ordinary Roman people who saw vast treasures from all over the world coming into the city. The empire extended itself for economic and business reasons. Those who mainly profited were the upper-rich social classes and landowners. However, there was always the danger that the ordinary people would riot or re-volt when they saw so much coming to Rome and realized they would have so little a share in it. Consequently, the emperors personally supervised periodic large distributions of grain and bread for the people as a special bounty from Caesar's hand. For entertainment there was the ancient Circus Maximus and the Coliseum which was completed before the time of Luke's Gospel. Thousands of gladiators as well as animals lost their lives in battles and feats of daring to provide diversion for the people.

However, in the story of Jesus' birth to bring "Peace on Earth," Luke focuses on the manger, a simple wooden feeding box for animals; the evangelist uses the word three times. First, Mary gave birth and "laid him in a *manger*" (2:7). Then an angel of the Lord tells the shepherds, *"This will be a sign for you:* you will find a child wrapped in bands of cloth and lying in a *manger"* (2:12). Third, the shepherds came and found Mary and Joseph and the child lying in a *manger* (2:16).

A sign often points to a mysterious meaning found in the Scriptures, the book of God's hidden plans. The word "manger" is rare but found a special place in the opening verses of the greatest prophet Isaiah, who is quoted more than any other in the New Testament. Speaking in God's name, Isaiah writes, "I have reared children and brought them up, but they have rebelled against me. The ox knows its owner, and the donkey its master's *manger*, but Israel does not know, my people do not understand."

The donkey had the reputation of being the dumbest, yet really the smartest of animals. Unlike some humans, it knows where to go for food—to the manger of its master (Lord). So the shepherds and the gospel audience, seeing the divine child in the manger can understand that this child is their real bread and source of nourishment. Luke carries the theme of sharing spiritual and physical bread throughout his Gospel and again balances the Gospel ending with the beginning. There, as we have previously described, two disciples on the way to Emmaus finally have their eyes opened and recognize Jesus in the breaking of bread at supper (Luke 24:31). Then Jesus appears to the eleven and others with his final greeting, "Peace be with you" (24:36).

Luke has already been preparing for this central theme of bread in his Gospel. In her *Magnificat*, Mary proclaims that God has filled the hungry with good things and sent the rich empty away (1:33). In the baptismal ministry of the Baptist, when the crowds ask him what they are to do, he responds that they should share food with those who have none (3:11). However, we do not get a glimpse as to how this is done until the story of Jesus' temptation.

"ONE DOES NOT LIVE BY BREAD ALONE":
GOD'S PROGRAM FOR EQUAL BREAD SHARING

After Jesus was baptized, he retired to the desert for prayer and serious decisions. When he had finished fasting and praying for forty days, he was famished with hunger. Then "The devil said to him, 'If you are the Son of God, command this stone to become a loaf of bread.'" Jesus answered him, "It is written, 'One does not live by bread alone'" (4:3-4). To understand Jesus' reply, we need to know, as the gospel audience did, its context as a quotation from Deuteronomy 8:2-3:

> Remember the long way that the LORD your God has led you these forty years in the wilderness, in order to humble you, *testing* you to know what was in your heart, whether or not you would keep his commandments. He humbled you by letting you hunger, then by feeding you with manna, with which neither you nor your ancestors were acquainted, in order to make you understand that *one does not live by bread alone, but by every word that comes from the mouth of the LORD* (8:2-3).

These verses show that the main concern is not just bread but following God's instructions (word) about the meaning and use of bread. This can be explained by going to the context of this statement in the story of the manna distribution to the Israelites in the Sinai desert. At that time, the people complained to God that they were dying of hunger. In response, God promised to send them bread they could gather up each day. As in the Deuteronomy text above, it is a test about whether they will follow God's commands: "In that way I will test them, whether they will follow my instruction or not" (Exod 16:4). Accordingly, on the morning God promised, the people found a white bread-like substance on the ground. Moses said to them,

> *This is what the LORD has commanded:* "Gather as much of it as each of you needs, an omer to a person according to the number of persons, all providing for those in their own tents." The Israelites did so, some gathering more, some less. But when they

measured it with an omer, those who gathered much had nothing over, and those who gathered little had no shortage; they gathered as much as each of them needed (Exod 16:16-18).

The italicized first sentence above is literally, "This is the *word* which the LORD has commanded." Thus it corresponds literally to "the word which comes from the mouth of God" in Deuteronomy 8:3 and also the all important Word of God in creation. In Genesis ch. 1 we have the phrase, "And God said" eight times. God does not want to just "rain down bread from *heaven*" (Exod 16:4). He wants people to be co-creators with him on *earth* to ensure that bread is equally shared by everyone. In view of the account that follows, each day God provided enough bread to be shared equally if the people followed his instructions.

When the people went out to gather bread in the morning, "some gathered more, some less." Perhaps the elderly and children were only able to gather a little, while the young and sturdy gathered large amounts. At the end of the day they divided it up equally. As a result, "those who gathered much had nothing over, and those who gathered little had no shortage; they gathered as much as each of them needed." This resulted in a great miracle of sharing and distribution according to the axiom, "From each one according to their ability; to each one according to their need." This has been attributed to Karl Marx and communism, but it is derived from the Bible.

Moses then said, "Let no one leave any of it over until morning." Here we note the effects of not following God's command through Moses. Those who distrusted and hoarded up for the future woke up in the morning and found worms eating their bread. In memory of the whole event, God commanded that some of the manna be placed beside the Ark of the Covenant (16:32). In Hebrew and Jewish tradition this miracle of distribution was regarded as even greater than the bread itself. St. Paul recalls it as a model of equal sharing for his ecumenical collection (2 Cor 8:13-15).

Luke in the Acts of the Apostles recalls the Deuteronomy plan of eliminating poverty and the ideal of sharing according to each one's need and the ability of others to help. He wrote, "There was not a needy person among them, for as many as owned lands or houses sold them and brought the proceeds of what was sold. They laid it at the apostles' feet, and it was distributed to each as any had need" (4:34-35). The last phrase, "to each as any had need" appears to be from the triple repeated phrase "as much as each needed" in Exod 16:16, 17, 21.

For Jesus, the devil's temptation was for him to obtain miraculous bread for himself alone regardless of God's command to have the gift of bread shared equally by all. This will help us understand the meaning of the Jesus' multiplication of bread for five thousand people in Luke 9:12-17. In that story the day was coming to a close and the disciples were concerned about having sufficient food as well as lodging for the people in some town near by. So they asked Jesus to send the crowds away to obtain food and shelter. We place below what follows for easy reference:

> But he (Jesus) said to them, "You give them something to eat." They said, "We have no more than five loaves and two fish—unless we are to go and buy food for all these people." For there were about five thousand men. And he said to his disciples, "Make them sit down in groups of about fifty each." They did so and made them all sit down. And taking the five loaves and the two fish, he looked up to heaven, and blessed and broke them, and gave them to the disciples to set before the crowd. And all ate and were filled. What was left over was gathered up, twelve baskets of broken pieces (9:13-17).

We note the following similarities to the Exodus story about the manna. Both occur in a desert place where people are hungry and far from their homes. The disciples express the people's need to Jesus just as the Israelites went to Moses. Jesus replied in what seems to be an impossible command, "*You* give them to eat" (9:13). This is an emphatic "you, yourselves" in Greek. They answered (after searching, according to Mark's Gospel) that they only have five loaves and two fishes. In those days, there were no fast-food outlets. Travelers usually carried several pancake-sized loaves in a bag or in a belt. This is implied in Jesus' previous instructions to the apostles before a mission tour: they are not to carry bread with them but trust they will be given a good reception and hospitality along the way (9:3). So we presume there were some people who did have provisions which might not be visible to others.

Yet the power of Jesus and following his instructions makes possible the feeding of five thousand people. With the similarity to Exodus and the manna, it is likely that those who had provisions followed Jesus and the Twelve's example and started to share with others until everyone had enough. This in itself was a great miracle. The splitting of the multitude into smaller groups makes this sharing much easier and provides a more personal atmosphere. We will see later that it foreshadows the small group gatherings in homes in the Acts of the Apostles where they share their food.

Because Jesus is behind the loaves' multiplication, there is also a deeper sense of communion with his person and mission in the form of spiritual nourishment also. This will be brought out in the Last Supper in the next chapter. The enormous quantity left over hints at a mystery: It tells the gospel audience that the remaining bread is a new superabundant bread that they too can eat for nourishment. This is confirmed by similarities with the Acts of the Apostles in the distribution of food in the early Jerusalem community:

> With great power the apostles gave their testimony to the resurrection of the Lord Jesus, and great grace was upon them all. There was not a needy person among them, for as many as owned lands or houses sold them and brought the proceeds of what was sold. They laid it at the apostles' feet, and it was distributed to each as any had need (4:34-37).

In this passage we note that the grace of the resurrected Christ is present in the community. This prompts them to bring offerings to the apostles who in turn distribute them to those in need. This is the same procedure as in the distribution of bread to the five thousand.

THE LORD'S PRAYER IN LUKE: DAILY BREAD IN EXODUS 16 AND THE ACTS OF THE APOSTLES

However, Luke is concerned that the distribution of bread should not be a great periodic display as with Caesar's "bread and circuses." The hungry need bread each day. So Luke's Lord's prayer petition reads, "Give us *each day* our daily bread" (11:3). In comparison to Matthew 6:11, Luke has *each day*, in Greek, *kathēmeran*. This is related to the distribution of the manna to the people of Israel each day. God said to Moses, "I am going to rain bread from heaven for you, and *each day* the people shall go out and *gather enough for that day*. In that way I will test them, whether they will follow my instruction or not" (Exod 16:3). Accordingly the people went out each day to gather the manna and then divided it equally among all. However there were some distrustful souls who gathered more than enough for the day and kept some for the next—just in case. But on the following morning, to their surprise and punishment, they found that the left over bread was filled with worms (Exod 16:20).

The early Jerusalem community tried to make the distribution of bread for the poor and hungry a daily reality. We learn this when there was a feeling that some of the Greek speaking disciples were being neglected in favor of Aramaic speakers in "the *daily* distribution of food" (Acts 6:1). This appears related to the Lord's prayer in Luke regarding the giving of bread *each day* (11:3). The same expression also occurs in the daily gatherings of disciples in Jerusalem where they broke bread and shared it "with glad and sincere hearts" (Acts 2:46). These were not large gatherings but small groups in various houses.

BREAD IN COVENANT MEALS

Forgiveness and Association

During the paralytic's cure, Jesus declared that he had power on earth to forgive sins (5:24). This was followed by the most unlikely prospects as Jesus called Levi a tax collector to be a disciple.

Levi then put on a great dinner for Jesus and his disciples and invited also many of his fellow tax collectors and friends. Being together at a meal like this was a public sign of association, covenant, and acceptance. So the Pharisees and their scribes objected saying, "Why do you eat and drink with tax collectors and sinners?" (5:30). Criticism of this type of association is found elsewhere in Luke. Later, a Pharisee who invites Jesus to dinner complains that he has allowed a woman of the city to approach and wash his feet at table. The Pharisee said to himself that if Jesus was a prophet, he would surely know that this woman is a sinner (7:39). Just before this story Jesus told his disciples that he was criticized for "eating and drinking" associations which prompted some people to say, "Look, a glutton and a drunkard, a friend of tax collectors and sinners" (7:34).

TEACHING ASSOCIATION AT MEALS

Many of Jesus' teachings take place in a meal environment. In addition, the loaves' multiplication is preceded by Jesus' teaching on the kingdom of God and by healings (9:11). Luke carefully places the loaves' story in a literary frame. It is preceded by Herod's question about who Jesus is and followed by the disciples' question and Peter's confession. This suggests that the teaching of Peter and the Twelve is connected with the meaning of the loaves. We will find the same connection in the Acts of the Apostles. After Pentecost, Luke notes that the newly baptized, "devoted themselves to the apostles' teaching, to the breaking of bread and the prayers" (2:42).

GRACE, PEACE, AND INVITATIONS TO MEALS

We have seen in chapter 11 that grace and invitation are prime themes in Luke as elements of true peace. I am reminded of a lecture many years ago by the great Scripture scholar Joachim Jeremias. After he had finished a very learned presentation he asked if there were any questions. A bright young student jumped to his feet and asked, "Professor Jeremias, would you give us a definition of 'grace'? The professor seemed nonplussed by this abrupt question. He hesitated for a moment and then said, "I can't give you a definition, but I can describe to you what it is like. It is like Jesus when he came near Jericho and looked up to see a little tax collector up in a tree and said to him, 'Zacchaeus, hurry up and come down. I must have dinner in your house today'" (adapted from 19:5). Dr. Jeremias actually had given the best definition possible. He illustrated that grace was not a theological construct but the exciting and beautiful feeling that comes from a personal invitation from Jesus.

Luke tries to reproduce this feeling in a series of invitation and banquet parables. "Invitation" or "call" is another favorite word-specialty of Luke. Three invitation parables are features in 14:7-24, each of them with the key word *invite* repeated three times. Jesus relates the first one as he notices guests pushing their way into the best seats of honor at a wedding banquet. Invitation and grace come to people who are humble and open. So if they act just the opposite by pushing their way ahead, they will only be humbled by being told to give up their seats to others. Jesus quotes the popular proverb, "For all who exalt themselves will be humbled, and those who humble themselves will be exalted" (14:11).

The second parable illustrates apparent but not real invitation or grace when invitations are those inspired by family duties or reciprocity. These have their own reward and do not need God's. So Jesus declares, "When you give a banquet, invite the poor, the crippled, the lame, and the blind. And you will be blessed, because they cannot repay you, for you will be repaid at the resurrection of the righteous" (14:13-14). Meals together should reflect Jesus' mission to the outcasts and those often excluded. Then they are truly God's banquets, not merely resulting from friendship or hope of return. They will receive the reward promised at the introduction when one of the dinner guests remarked, "Blessed is anyone who will eat bread in the kingdom of God!" (14:11).

The third parable reflects the urgency and unlimited inclusiveness of God's invitation to "eat bread in the kingdom of God." A certain man sent out special invitations to a great dinner. But all made excuses they could not come, some with apparently urgent ones like those which would even have freed them from biblical military service; for example a recent marriage (Deut 14:20). Among this first group, the Pharisee hosting Jesus' dinner must have been included. The master of the house was angry that his invitation was not accepted, but this only prompted him to search for others: the poor, crippled, blind, and lame that we saw in the first parable above.

Yet the master found there was still room in the feast and even sent his slaves outside the city. He told them: "Go out into the roads and lanes, and compel people to come in, so that my house may be filled. For I tell you, none of those who were (first) invited will taste my dinner" (14:23-24). The word "compel" has a bad history; it was used for centuries as a justification to force people into conversion. However it refers to the oriental custom of going as far as possible to convince guests to accept hospitality. This last group refers to the outsiders seen for example in Luke as Gentiles, Samaritans, and strangers. God's love and invitation to his heavenly banquet extends to all without exception.

SUMMARY

Beginning with the sign of the manger, Luke sees "Peace on Earth" as inculcated by Jesus as the source of spiritual and material bread. Jesus responds to Satan's temptation to produce bread to satisfy his hunger by appealing to Deuteronomy 8:3, "Not by bread alone." This refers to God's instructions in Exodus 16 about the daily and equal sharing of manna for the people. The miraculous multiplication and distribution of loaves can be better understood in view of this background. The Lord's prayer with its provision for bread *each day* reflects the manna distribution and serves as a model for the distribution of food *each day* for widows in Acts 6. Sharing of bread also had a special covenant meaning in regard to forgiveness and association with sinners. Invitation and grace connected with meals are characteristic of Jesus and his parables.

COROLLARY FOR TODAY

Getting back to basics, religion and faith today mean little without a priority given to feeding the hungry and poor. The problem is mostly distribution. This cannot be done by only "bread and circus" handouts and generosity. Luke's Gospel presents a model of meaningful small associations who learn to share equally what they have with one another. Forgiveness and acceptance cannot be on a standoff basis. They need the personal dimension that comes from sharing and breaking bread together. An acid test of the inclusiveness of love is found in the extent of the invitations we give to others. Outward demonstrations for peace are very important. However, they are truly genuine only to the extent that we "demonstrate" by practical action a sense of justice and compassion for the hungry, suffering, and needy.

Jesus' attitude in Luke was not limited to protests against violence or injustice. Otherwise, an attitude of waiting for evil to happen might result. Governments or leaders could take action knowing that they would not be preventing from doing what they want and that the protests would come post factum. Instead, practical initiatives of justice for the hungry and poor can accomplish peace by preventing war and violence.

13

Jesus' Last Passover Supper and Testament for Continuity

IN OUR LAST CHAPTER WE NOTED THAT MEALS WITH JESUS AND THE meaning of bread permeates Luke's Gospel. Breaking bread together usually signified a family covenant or association with Jesus as well as sharing with one another. Jesus' Last Supper will continue this meaning of covenant. All the gospel meals culminate in Jesus' last meal before his death, and then will continue in renewed meals with his disciples after his resurrection. Jesus' last meal focuses on his death and how his disciples will continue his mission and life style after his resurrection. Luke sees Jesus' death as modeled on that of the Passover lamb and sacrifice: "Then came the day of Unleavened Bread, on which the Passover lamb had to be sacrificed" (22:7). The word *had* implies a necessity in God's plans or the Scriptures. Jesus also begins the supper with a parallel between himself and the Passover lamb:

> When the hour came, he took his place at the table, and the apostles with him. He said to them, "I have eagerly desired to eat this Passover with you before I suffer; for I tell you, I will not eat it until it is fulfilled in the kingdom of God" (22:14-16).

"The hour" indicates a special time in God's plans like the hour when Jesus was arrested (22:53). The words "eagerly desired" express his long-standing deep desire and loving purpose. The connection between the Passover and his death is emphasized by a play on word sound. The Hebrew word *pesach* for "Passover" was transliterated into *pascha* in Greek. This in turn sounded like the verb *paschein*, "to suffer." However it also includes, at times, the idea of death as when Jesus makes his final address to his disciples before his ascension and says that the Scriptures indicate that the Messiah will *suffer* and rise from the dead. Jesus' words that he will no longer drink the fruit of the vine with them also indicate his death but with the additional promise of continuity: "Until it is fulfilled in the kingdom of God."

THE PASSOVER LAMB
AND THE MEANING OF JESUS' SACRIFICE

In general, the feast of Passover celebrated God's action in bringing his people freedom, especially from their slavery in Egypt. The Ten Commandments start with the words, "I am the LORD your God who brought you out of the land of Egypt, out of that house of slavery" (Exod 20:2-4). At that time the Hebrew people were threatened by a deadly plague that struck the whole land of Egypt. To save them, God commanded that each home sacrifice a lamb and sprinkle its blood over the doorway: "The blood shall be a sign for you on the houses where you live: when I see the blood, I will pass over you, and no plague shall destroy you when I strike the land of Egypt" (Exod 12:13). Following this, there was a family meal in which everyone ate part of the paschal lamb. The sacrifice of the lamb also represented the lives of the people themselves as a gift to God.

In regard to Jesus, a sacrifice meant following what God wanted of him, even if it resulted in death. So in this sense it would be giving his life to God. What God wanted of him was to follow his call to be a prophet. Jesus explained this specifically on one occasion when he was warned to flee from Herod the king. He answered, "Today, tomorrow, and the next day I must be on my way, because it is impossible for a prophet to be killed

outside of Jerusalem" (13:33). In other words, every prophet was
called upon to preach in the capital city. Yet this is the very place
where their lives were most in danger. The agony in the garden
is especially significant in this regard. It was Jesus' last chance to
return by night into Galilee where he had many faithful supporters. Only after hours of prayer he received the strength to
make his decision to face Judas and the cohort who would arrest
him and begin the process that would lead to his death.

Jesus continually warned his disciples about the dangers that
lay ahead and the need to be willing to face even the cross. In
Luke, this is especially emphasized with the addition of the word
"daily": "Then he [Jesus] said to them all, 'If any want to become
my followers, let them deny themselves and take up their cross
daily and follow me'" (9:23). Early in the Gospel, John the Baptist became a model because, as a prophet, he admonished King
Herod who later put him to death. The words of both Jesus and
the Baptist have special power because the risk of their lives is
behind them.

PARTICIPATION IN JESUS' SACRIFICE

> Then he took a cup, and after giving thanks he said, "Take this
> and divide it among yourselves; for I tell you that from now on
> I will not drink of the fruit of the vine until the kingdom of God
> comes." Then he took a loaf of bread, and when he had given
> thanks, he broke it and gave it to them, saying, "This is my body,
> *which is given for you. Do this in remembrance of me." And he
> did the same with the cup after supper, saying, "This cup that is
> poured out for you is the new covenant in my blood"* (22:17-20).

(The words italicized above represent the longer form
adopted in some ancient Greek manuscripts.) This does not
mean that they are later ideas. Actually they follow the earlier in-
stitution account found in St. Paul (1 Cor 11:23-26).

First, sharing the one cup signifies an active commitment to
share the meaning of Jesus' life and mission. Thus it is the cup of
the new covenant as in the second underlined text. The breaking

and sharing of the one loaf signifies the same. Eating as well as drinking belong to the fullness of meals with Christ that will later be repeated. The significance of the whole action is essential, not a static matter of the bread separately and the wine. However, the blood poured out especially points to his death. The double use of the expression "given for you" or "for you" bring out the personal and dedicated giving of Jesus' self that he wants his disciples to imitate.

The whole ritual has an empowering as well as nourishing aspect. All of God's power is present in Jesus' action to give himself to his mission even as far as the death that made it a sacrifice. Those joined to Jesus share in that power through their communion and association with him. Finally, the words "Do this in remembrance of me" have special meaning. The Passover celebration was called a feast of perpetual remembrance (Exod 12:14). Even in later generations, when children asked about its meaning the parents were to reply, "It is the Passover sacrifice to the LORD, for he passed over the houses of the Israelites in Egypt, when he struck down the Egyptians but spared our houses" (Exod 12:7). *Our houses* refers to the continued present experience in every generation.

So for Jesus, these words indicate that all he has done will be continually reexperienced, relived, and reproduced in the lives of all who celebrate his memory. They will continue Jesus' mission with his presence and power. Jesus makes this succession motif more explicit by adding "You are those who have stood by me in my trials; and I confer on you, just as my Father has conferred on me, a kingdom, so that you may eat and drink at my table in my kingdom, and you will sit on thrones judging the twelve tribes of Israel" (22:28-30). The *twelve tribes* were the descendants and successors of their father Jacob/Israel. The *twelve* apostles, representing Jesus' community, are the new community (after Israel) taking Jesus' place.

Luke explains this new community three times by the verb "redeem" or the noun "redemption," only used in his Gospel (of the four). They are the first words when the Holy Spirit opens the mouth of Zechariah to bless the God of Israel because (literally) "he has visited and redeemed his people" (1:68). The prophet Anna comes into the Temple and speaks about the child Jesus to all who were awaiting "the redemption of Israel" (1:38). In a gospel closing episode the two disciples say to the mysterious stranger (Jesus in disguise) that they were hoping "that he was the one to redeem Israel" (24:21). The word "redemption" means to reacquire or reestablish the covenant of God with his people as promised by the prophets. So the words of Jesus at the supper "the cup of the new covenant" (22:20) have special significance.

JESUS' FURTHER EXPLANATION OF THE MEANING AND SPIRIT OF HIS SUPPER FOR PARTICIPANTS

First, Jesus' community will continue on despite every possible obstacle present or future even the worst betrayals engineered by the devil. The devil had entered Judas at the beginning of the passion narrative (22:3). Yet despite this Jesus declares, "But see, the one who betrays me is with me, and his hand is on the table. For the Son of Man is going as it has been determined, but woe to that one by whom he is betrayed!" (22:21-22). In other words, Jesus will go on, as well as his disciples, despite the opposition of the devil even in the betrayal of close friends.

Yet even the betrayal by Judas is not as great as that of Peter succumbing to the temptations of the evil one: Jesus tells Peter, "Simon, Simon, listen! Satan has demanded to sift all of you like wheat, but I have prayed for you that your own faith may not fail; and you, when once you have turned back, strengthen your brothers" (22:31-32). Because of Jesus' prayer and support, even the failure of Peter and his repentance will make it possible for him to confirm others in their faith.

This whole context of betrayal, especially the mention of temptation and the devil brings up an important issue regarding power and authority in the community. Jesus' presence will not be shown by domination and lording it over others:

A dispute also arose among them as to which one of them was regarded as the greatest. But Jesus said to them, "The kings of the Gentiles lord it over them; and those in authority over them are called benefactors. But not so with you; rather the greatest among you must become like the youngest, and the leader like one who serves. For who is greater, the one who is at the table or the one who serves? Is it not the one at the table? But I am among you as one who serves" (22:25-27).

The word "dispute" that Luke uses here is a very strong one used rarely in the Bible. It implies a sharp division—the very opposite of the covenant of peace in the Last Supper. Only Luke reports this incident at the Last Supper, while the other evangelists have it elsewhere. Luke is writing some fifty years or more after Jesus' Last Supper. So he must have placed it here as a real issue in the life of the Church as some members tried to dominate over others. Competition for places of power over others is a very human failing. Jesus replies to this by stating that there should be real competition for the most humble service of others. For in doing so, a disciple becomes most like the master.

The Gospel of Luke has the strongest theme in the New Testament about becoming like little children. So Jesus states that those who wish to be "greatest" as "elders" should become like the youngest and that the true leader is one who serves. In the Acts of the Apostles, Luke has the twelve apostles take these instructions seriously. Although there is a daily distribution of goods and food for the widows, the Twelve do not merely supervise it. They actually wait on tables themselves to place a priority on serving with their own hands (6:1-2). In the Last Supper, the Twelve took no mediator or supervisory role. Jesus himself was the priest who offered himself as a victim to God. Luke's account of the Last Supper thus includes the model and spirit of those who participate as servants of one another, not as people using force, violence, or power over others. In the garden, Jesus declared that this was a characteristic of the power of darkness (22:53).

After the resurrection, when Jesus first appeared to the assembled disciples, he greeted them as customary with the words, "Peace be with you" (24:36). Even though these words are not in some Greek manuscripts they would certainly have been his greeting. Since the disciples were terrified at this sight, Jesus showed them his hands and his feet. The previously ugly wounds had now become glorious signs of his identity and characteristic I.D. of his disciples. Jesus the priest bears the marks of himself as crucified and sacrificial victim. After that he entrusted his disciples to continue his own mission "that repentance and forgiveness of sins is to be proclaimed in his name to all nations beginning with Jerusalem" (24:47). To be able to do so, he then tells them to wait in the city until they receive his own spirit and power: "See, I am sending upon you what my Father promised me; so stay here in the city until you have been clothed on high" (24:49).

After every sacrifice in the Temple priestly enclosure, the priest would come out to bless the people. The people anxiously awaited this for it was a transfer of the divine energy that came from the sacrifices. So Jesus as priest also closes the Gospel with a blessing: "Then he led them as far as Bethany, and lifting up hands, he blessed them" (24:50). The last wording of this special priestly blessing given directly by God were, "The LORD lift up his countenance upon you and give you *peace*" (Num 6:26). Thus Jesus' last word in the Gospel is *peace*, matching the first proclamation concerning him as a child, *peace on earth*. The blessing for the audience that was missed in the beginning because of Zechariah's uncertainty, now is given to the gospel readers/listeners at the end.

SUMMARY

The meals with Jesus in the Gospel culminate in the Last Supper with a special focus on Jesus' sacrifice, death, and resurrection. A covenant meal of bread and wine enables disciples to unite themselves with Jesus in this event. As his Last Testament, Jesus wishes his disciples to continue to celebrate that supper in memory of him. This will nourish and empower them to continue his mission. Luke adds references to the betrayal of Peter and Judas to assure them that nothing will hinder Jesus or his disciples to continue that mission. The spirit of the Last Supper must be that of humble service of one another, avoiding the diabolic temptation to use force, domination, and power over others.

COROLLARY FOR TODAY

"Today" is the same as the "Today" for Luke in his own time. Human nature has not changed, but the predominance of churches as large institutions makes application even more difficult. Jesus told his disciples as a last testament that they must not adopt secular models of authority adopted by kings and rulers who use coercive means to gain compliance. There are no easy solutions to avoid this but there is need to constantly look at ourselves in the mirror and spirit of the Gospels, that of humble service. Children today quickly learn the competitive spirit in school when they discover they must strive to get grades that would surpass others. Recently a local newspaper printed an excerpt of a graduation address (June 2002) by Fred Rogers, a children's television pioneer who will always remain in every child's memory as "Mr. Rogers."

> Have you heard the story that came out of the Seattle Special Olympics? For the 100-yard dash there were nine contestants, all of them so-called physically or mentally disabled. All nine of them assembled at the starting line and at the sound of the gun they took off. But one little boy didn't get too far. He stumbled and fell and hurt his knee and began to cry.

> The other eight children heard the boy crying. They slowed down, turned around and ran back to him—every one of them ran back to him. One little girl with Down syndrome bent down and kissed the boy and said, "This will make it better." The little boy got up, and he and the rest of the runners linked their arms together and joyfully walked to the finish line.

They all finished the race at the same time. And when they did, everyone in the stadium stood up and clapped and whistled and cheered for a long, long time. People who were there are still telling the story with obvious delight. And do you know why? Because deep down we know that what matters in this life is more than winning for ourselves. What really matters is helping others win, too, even if it means slowing down and changing our course now and then.

14

Jesus' Compassion for Animals: A First Step Toward a Nonviolent World

LUKE COULD BE CALLED THE "GOSPEL OF ANIMALS." HE MENTIONS them more than any other Gospel and gives more attention to Jesus' own compassion for them. In our last chapter, we saw how Luke's Gospel begins with Jesus' genealogy going back to Adam and Eve in Paradise. After their disobedience, a "cosmic combat" began with Satan to reverse the closure of the Garden of Eden. Finally, it was reopened on the cross when Jesus promised the repented criminal that he would enter a reopened Paradise together with him. The image that Luke and Jesus had of Paradise included the animals. God brought each of the animals before Adam so he could name them (Gen 2:19-20). This implied a special relationship with them. In addition, the prophet Isaiah described a renewed world of peace that included a recovered harmonious association with the animals:

> The wolf shall live with the lamb, the leopard shall lie down with the kid, the calf and the lion and the fatling together, and a little child shall lead them. The cow and the bear shall graze, their young shall lie down together; and the lion shall eat straw like the ox (Isa 11:6-8).

THE ROOTS OF JESUS' COMPASSION
FOR ANIMALS IN LUKE

God's Rachum *for Animals*

In the Sermon on the Plain, Jesus was the supreme model for a believer: "Be merciful just as your Father is merciful" (6:36). We have seen in chapter 6 that this "mercy" is meaning of God's name as revealed to Moses. The first quality or attribute of God is that of his *rachum* or womb-compassion (Exod 34:6). This compassion of God extends not only to people but to animals. The Psalms extend this love and compassion to all without distinction. Psalm 145 has been a daily prayer for Israel for many centuries. It sets the general principle in the words, "The LORD is gracious and merciful, *rachum*, slow to anger and abounding in steadfast love. The LORD is good to all, and his compassion, *rachum*, is over all his works" (vv. 8-9). Also, "The eyes of all look to you, and you give them their food in due season. You open your hand, satisfying the desire of every living thing" (vv. 16-17).

Psalm 146 gives specifics, "He gives to animals their food and to the young ravens when they cry" (9). In response, Psalm 148 calls on the whole world to praise the Lord. This includes, "Wild animals and all cattle, creeping things and flying birds" (149:10). God's loving care for animals also stems from his creative work. Animals always belong to him and claim his attention and mercy: "Every wild animal of the forest is mine, the cattle on a thousand hills; I know all the birds of the air, and all that moves in the field is mine" (Ps 50:10-11).

Another example of God's *rachum* is found in the book of Jonah, which was the subject of chapter 10, but here we add details about the animals. The prophet Jonah had been sent to preach to Nineveh, capital of Assyria, the most brutal enemy the Israelites ever had. Jonah told them that in forty days the city would be overturned. The king set the example of repentance for the whole people by leaving his throne, putting on sackcloth, and sitting in ashes. Then the king proclaimed, "No human being or animal, no herd or flock, shall taste anything. They shall not feed, nor shall they drink water. Human beings and animals shall be covered with sackcloth, and they shall cry mightily to God. All shall turn from their evil ways and from the violence that is in their hands" (3:7-8).

The king also decreed, "All shall turn from their evil ways and from the violence that is in their hands." The book of Jonah is of course, comic literature and we are not to imagine animals actually putting on sack cloth. But the text is meant to show the close association between animals and human beings. Actually the animals were also guilty of violence by their cooperation in Assyrian violent warfare. The author in the text above actually has both animals and humans crying out to God in prayer. As a result, God "changed his mind" and spared even the Assyrians. However, Jonah did not change his mind and was very angry that God did not punish Israel's greatest enemy. Jonah himself had not renounced the violence that he wished the Assyrians to repent. He complained to God that this was why he had fled to Spain to avoid preaching: "For I knew that you were a gracious God and merciful, *rachum*" (4:2).

When Jonah persisted in his anger and even wanted to die, God taught him a lesson. Jonah became very concerned when a little shade tree dried up that sheltered him from the sweltering heat. But God said, "Should I not be concerned about Nineveh, that great city, in which there are more than a hundred and twenty thousand persons who do not know their right hand from their left, and also *many animals?*" Children and the many animals are the last words in the book to show God's loving concern about all his little ones.

COMPASSION FOR ANIMALS IN BIBLICAL LAW AND TRADITION

This compassion is highlighted in the Biblical Covenant and Tradition. Jesus' own views are first of all based on the Ten Commandments and the connected covenant provisions of Mount Sinai. The Ten Commandments form the core of God's covenant and contain special provisions for animals. The tenth commandment reads: "Neither shall you desire your neighbor's house, or field, or male or female slave or ox or donkey, or anything that belongs to your neighbor" (Deut 5:21). This commandment treats the ox and the donkey as precious parts of the household with the same guaranteed security and protection given to human beings.

The fourth commandment reads: "The Sabbath day is a Sabbath to the LORD your God; you shall not do any work—you, or your son or your daughter, or your male or female slave, or your ox or donkey, or any of your livestock, or the resident alien in your towns, so that your male and female slave may rest as well as you" (Deut 5:12-14). Thus domestic animals were to receive the same privileges as human beings. In Jewish tradition, many stories were handed down about animals who were sold or transferred to Gentile owners and then refused to work on the Sabbath! This is not unlikely since animals are very much creatures of routine.

The covenant following the Ten Commandments spells out how animals should be treated. For example, in regard to stray animals: No one should simply watch a neighbor's ox, sheep, or donkey straying and do nothing about it. They should take the animals back to their owners. If they can't be found, the animals should be cared for until the owner claims them (Deut 22:1-2). This applies even if the owner is your enemy (Exod 23:4). The important matter is care for the animal. Mere inaction is reprehensible. A law like this was regarded as extending to similar cases of lost or straying animals. This has become an increasing problem today. In the United States alone there are about fifty million cats and an equal number of dogs. Every day a large number are simply abandoned when owners move to new locations or are unable to care for them any longer. The basic compassion for animals at the roots of the biblical law is needed so people can give more attention to the rescue of stray cats and dogs.

THE SPECIAL PRIORITY OF ANIMALS IN PAIN

"You shall not see your neighbor's donkey or ox fallen on the road and ignore it; you shall help to lift it up" (Deut 22:4). Once again, the law applies even if the animal belongs to an enemy. The focus is on the pain of the animal. Mere standing or watching by is inexcusable. Humans must exercise compassion in action.

"You shall not plow with an ox or donkey yoked together" (Deut 22:10). This is because the weaker donkey would suffer beside a much stronger animal pulling the same yoke. "You shall not muzzle an ox while it is treading grain" (Deut 25:4). The continual pain here is the animal's pangs of hunger at work, yet muzzled so it can never taste any of the grain beneath its feet that could give it strength and nourishment. In both these cases, the owner should exercise watchful compassion, alert to what animals are feeling.

"When an ox or a sheep or a goat is born, it shall remain seven days with its mother [before being taken away for food or sacrifice]" (Lev 22:26). This was out of compassion for the feelings of its mother on being so quickly deprived of its offspring. And also of the helpless calf deprived of a mother's nourishment and protection. The basis of this law needs to be applied to modern "factory" practices of separating animals from their young almost immediately after birth.

Biblical laws such as these gave rise to a principle for action called THE PAIN OF LIVING BEINGS. This meant that a person should never act in a way that would cause pain to any living being, whether a human or an animal. Jewish tradition applied this in regard to feeding animals: they should be fed before sitting down to eat one's own meal. Our cat seems to have found out about this and usually sits down beside our table just as we are getting ready to eat! Jesus applied the "pain of living beings principle" when it came to the question of whether healing was allowed on the Sabbath.

JESUS' PRINCIPLE: COMPASSION FOR ANIMALS SUPERSEDES OTHER LAWS

Even though prohibition of work on the Sabbath was the third of the Ten Commandments, compassion for animals superseded it. The Sabbath observation and laws were at the heart of Judaism. Yet people generally recognized that care of animals and concern for their pain took priority over these laws. Jesus knew this well and emphasized it on two occasions in regard to healing on the Sabbath. The first was the healing of a crippled woman who could no longer stand up straight. In reply to objections that she should be cured on another day than the Sabbath, Jesus stated, "Does not each of you on the Sabbath untie his ox or donkey from the manger and lead it to give it water?" (Luke 13:15). In this story Jesus plays on the word "untie." He unties the bound up woman just as they untie an ox or a donkey. He unties the Sabbath laws so they yield to compassion for both humans and animals. In a second Sabbath healing, Jesus echoes the same motif in response to silent criticism. He tells them, "If one of you has a donkey or an ox that has fallen into a well, will you not immediately pull it out on a Sabbath day?" (Luke 14:5).

JESUS AND ANIMALS RAISED FOR FOOD

Luke's Fatted Calf

The story of the prodigal son is so familiar that the centrality of the family and community meal is often forgotten. Luke introduced three related parables of loss and restoration by citing the complaint to Pharisees and scribes: "This fellow welcomes sinners and eats with them" (15:2). In each of the first two parables, the conclusion is the calling together of friends and neighbors to rejoice over the finding of a lost sheep or a lost coin. This is an application of the biblical precept about the priority for lost animals.

In the third parable of the prodigal son, the beloved home pet, the fatted calf, becomes central to the story and is mentioned three times (15:23-30). The first reference is the father's orders to prepare a great party celebration: He tells his servants: "Get the fatted calf and slaughter it, and let us eat and celebrate." The second is when the servants report to the older brother what is going on: They tell him, "Your brother has come and your father has killed the fatted calf." The third expresses the resentment of the older son as he tells his father that he has never been feasted even with a young goat, but now his younger brother who has squandered his father's money gets a fatted calf.

Here we notice the custom that eating meat is limited to special occasions. The fatted calf had been raised in free, pleasant surroundings and had enjoyed a good life. It would be unthinkable to permit such an animal to suffer. The animal is not just a "thing" destined for future hamburgers but a related and respected living being who will always be beloved and remembered. Only animals such as this could be said to "give their lives" to be part of a family feast on a special occasion.

This view is directly opposite to the way that over 90 percent of our meat comes to us. The U.S. Food and Drug Administration describes this as following:

> Animal feeding operations (AFOs) are agricultural enterprises where animals are kept and raised in confined situations. AFOs cluster animals, feed, manure and urine, dead animals and production operations on a small area. Feed is brought to the animals rather than the animals grazing or otherwise seeking feed in pastures, fields, or on rangeland. There are approximately 450,000 AFOs in the United States. Common types of AFOs include dairies, cattle feedlots, chicken and hog farms (USFDA/EPA 1999).

In addition, the fatted calf or any such animal was carefully protected by biblical law from the time of its birth. Out of compassion for the mother and concern for the calf, the newly born animal had to remain at least seven days with its mother after birth (Lev 22:26). Such concerns are not antiquarian. In Luke's Gospel the fatted calf has been first raised close to its mother and nourished by her warm milk and affection. Then it has been close to the family and household as a special pet. It knows its destiny as being raised for a special family occasion. When it does come to the family table in such an event, it brings not only physical nourishment but all the memories of its happy and free life.

The ethical requirements of the Hebrew Scriptures were never abrogated by Christianity. However, in most modern "factory farming," calves destined for veal are almost immediately taken away from their mothers despite the anguish, grief, and suffering of both animals. Then the calf is closely confined and fed so it will furnish tender cutlets. Approximately 1.5 million calves each year in the United States are born and raised in this way. Those who are conscious of this usually make an ethical choice not to foster such treatment by eating such foods whether at home or in a restaurant.

A Hen with Her Chicks—A Teaching Image of Jesus' Compassion

On one occasion some Pharisees warned Jesus to go away since Herod was seeking to kill him. Jesus replied that he must be on his way to Jerusalem because every prophet was called to preach in the nation's capital even at the risk of their lives. He said, "Jerusalem, Jerusalem, the city that kills the prophets and stones those who are sent to it! How often have I desired to gather your children together *as a hen gathers her brood under her wings* and you were not willing" (Luke 13:34). In using this simile, Jesus was taking a favorite image of God's own protection of his people. The Psalmist prays, "Guard me as the apple of the eye; hide me in the shadow of your wings" (17:8; also 57:1; 61:4). In the Roman world also, the hen was especially esteemed for her example of maternal love and care.

At the time of Jesus, poultry and eggs were very important for food production. However the image is that of a hen free to walk around in the open air and sunshine as well as allowed to reproduce and take care of her little ones. She had a normal good and unconfined life before she was on the dinner table. When that time came, she had to be slaughtered according to special laws that guaranteed that this be done quickly and without pain. Slaughtering became a profession where only sensitive and respected people were allowed to enter so they would offer no unnecessary pain to animals.

However, today, Jesus' image has become obsolete in factory farms, some so large that they hold a million chickens tightly confined in cages and raised in great physical and psychological torment. Each year in the United States about 7.5 billion chickens are slaughtered and over 90 percent in those factory conditions. Poultry are even exempt from the minimum requirements of avoiding suffering that are provided by the Federal Humane Slaughtering Act of 1978. (This is because of a legal technicality that chickens are birds not animals!)

Fortunately, there are now more and more opportunities to buy and eat "range-free" chickens as well as "cage-free" eggs. This provides the option to follow the biblical directive of (avoiding) "The pain of living beings" that Jesus himself respected. The food industries are the largest in the world, commanding tens of billions of dollars in resources. Yet they have an Achilles heel and are extremely vulnerable because even one choice in a store, at home, or in a restaurant can lead others to follow and demand meats of animals raised and slaughtered without suffering.

Although the mother hen is rarely seen now with her little chicks following her, she has become a nourishing mother of humanity. She now furnishes the world with 80 percent of its meat supply and about seventy billion eggs a year. It is encouraging to see that some egg cartons are now labeled not only "cage free" but fertilized and organic as well. So at least these hens have the benefit of rooster companions and the first thrills of procreation! Making the choice to buy this type of egg is a contribution toward "female liberation" in the poultry world!

In conclusion, Luke's presentation of Jesus' concern and respect for animals helps us appreciate them as teachers who prevent us from becoming mere robots in our rapidly moving technological world. The prime characteristic of a robot is lack of compassion. Each day, the animals call out to teach us that compassion. An ancient rabbi used to say, "If the Torah had not done so, the animals would have taught us compassion." Each personal choice whether at table or at a market makes a vast difference and encourages others to do the same. At stake are the lives and sufferings each year of the following animals in the United States alone: approximately 7.5 billion chickens, 97 million pigs, 36 million cows, 5 million sheep and lambs, 1.5 million veal calves. All together this means about 22 million animals each day, almost a million an hour, around 170,000 a minute!

WAS JESUS A VEGETARIAN?

Christians have always taken Jesus as a supreme ethical model to follow. His first words in his call to his first disciples in Matthew and Mark were, "Come follow me" (4:18; 1:17). However, Jesus, as a practicing Jew, could not have been a vegetarian. Like everyone else, he observed the Passover celebration. The rules for the feast called for eating the Passover lamb. God's command to the people was, "They shall eat the lamb that same night" (Exod 12:8). Also, we have seen in Jesus' parable of the prodigal son that the eating of the fatted calf had a central place in the joyful celebration. In Jesus' parable of the wedding feast he describes the king (who represents God) as saying, "My oxen and fat calves have been slaughtered, and everything is ready; come to the wedding feast" (Matt 22:4). It is doubtful the invitation would have included an optional vegetarian diet. It must be kept in mind also, that meat was not part of the daily diet of the Hebrew people. It was a luxury for special occasions. In addition, they did not usually have dogs or cats as household pets. Instead, there was a close bond with sheep, calves, and various household animals. This made people reluctant to slaughter them except for special occasions.

As for fish, all the Gospels describe Jesus as multiplying both bread and fish to give to the crowds. Luke tells us that Jesus himself ate a piece of broiled fish to confirm the reality of his presence in his last appearance to his disciples (24:42). Eggs too contribute to an acceptable diet. Jesus illustrated the goodness of a father who would not give a child a scorpion when an egg was requested (Luke 11:12).

However if Jesus were in today's world (and he is, in Christian belief), it would be difficult for him *not* to be a vegetarian, at least in regard to meat. His own compassion for animals (as well as biblical laws) would keep him from knowingly eating or cooperating in any way with the suffering and torture undergone by any of the 90 percent or more of animals raised for food production in the United States alone.

The book of Job reminds us about how nature and in particular the animals are some of our best teachers: *Ask the animals and they will teach you; the birds of the air and they will tell you; ask the plants of the earth and they will teach you; and the fish of the sea will declare to you* (12:10). What we eat, our choices at table, and how animals are treated play an essential role in making us who we are meant to be—people of peace. The animals were in Paradise, the Garden of Eden before us. We cannot return there without them.

15

Spiritual Combat for Peace: The Power of the Holy Spirit and Prayer

SCIENCE HAS CONTINUED TO DEMONSTRATE THE CLOSE INTERCON-nections among all living beings and the interchange of energy that is continually taking place. The ancient world called these energies by the Greek word *dynamis*. This is the *inner* world that Luke's Gospel takes for granted. Jesus teaches that each individual has an important part to play in it and can influence it through prayer and meditation. Because true peace can only come from God, the Psalmist tells us: "Pray for the peace of Jerusalem" (122:6). Here the Hebrew has a sound play on the same last consonants as "Jerusalem" and the word for "peace," *shalom*. Jesus must have thought of these words when he approached Jerusalem for the last time and wept over the city with the prayerful lament, "If you, even you had only recognized on this day the things that make for *peace*" (19:41). Jesus saw himself in conflict with those who looked for military messiahs and spoke so differently. He must have felt like the Psalmist who again wrote, "I am for peace; but when I speak they are for war" (120:7).

In our last chapter we noted the close connection between justice and peace. As the Messiah of peace, Jesus' prayers must have been focused often on this area. An example of his prayerful concern for justice is found in his parable of the persevering widow who continually came to an unjust judge asking for justice.

The judge could not care less and kept putting her off. Finally, he said to himself, "Because this widow keeps bothering me, I will grant her justice, so that she may not wear me out by continually coming" (18:5). Then Jesus said, "Listen to what the unjust judge says. And will not God grant *justice* to his chosen ones who cry to him day and night?" Jesus is instructing the gospel audience that persevering prayer for justice and peace is a daily priority.

THE PRAYER LIFE OF JESUS

"Desert Spirituality" in Luke

The desert was a place where this *dynamis* of prayer and the Holy Spirit was most available and active. By "desert" is not meant an area like the Sahara but a wilderness or a quiet, usually uninhabited place where a person could go for undisturbed meditation or prayer. The word "desert" in Greek is *erēmos*. From this root we derive the words, "eremite" or "hermit." Luke has this word twelve times, more than any other gospel. The desert has a long meaningful tradition in the Bible. The beginning of God's covenant took place in the desert of Sinai where God revealed his name to Moses (Exod 3:13-15). On Sinai, God gave the Ten Commandments to his people (Exod 20:1-17).

The Hebrew people spent forty years in this desert peninsula before entering the promised land. The desert (often translated "wilderness") was frequently recalled as a place both of their espousal with God and also temptation. God tells the people through Jeremiah, "I remember the devotion of your youth, your love as a bride, how you followed me in the wilderness" (2:2). The desert could also function as a place for renewal. The great prophet Elijah returned there for strength when Queen Jezebel tried to impose the Baal fertility worship on Israel (1 Kgs 19:1-18).

John the Baptist and the Desert

As a youth, John had learned from his father that his mission was "to guide our feet into the way of peace" (1:79). The Baptist spent much time in the desert until the time of his public ministry began: "He was in the desert until the day he appeared publicly in Israel" (1:80). There the Word of God and his prophetic call first came to him (3:1). It was a fulfillment of the prophet Isaiah promising a chosen messenger of God crying in the *desert* to prepare the way of the Lord (3:4). People came from afar to the wilderness area around the Jordan to listen to his preaching and receive his baptism. Jesus later said of him, "What did you go out into the wilderness to look at? A reed shaken by the wind?" (7:24). Jesus came to John in the desert for his own baptism and joined him in ministry there until Herod imprisoned John and waited for a suitable time to execute him (3:18).

Jesus and the Desert

After his baptism, Jesus retired to the desert for an intensive period of prayer and decision-making. The desert was also a wild and dangerous place in biblical tradition. Israel was tempted there for forty years before being allowed to enter the promised land. The desert was also a haunt for wild animals and devils. Luke describes Jesus as driving the Gerasene demons back into the desert (8:29). This dangerous aspect of the desert is part of human experience. When people are alone and quiet, the "devils within" tend to jump out and confront them about realities they are not facing in themselves.

While with the Baptist, Jesus had seen many people coming to the desert but decided that this was not enough. He decided to "bring the desert" out to the world rather than bring the world to the desert. When crowds came searching for Jesus trying to make him a local healer, he avoided them at daybreak by going to a desert place (4:42). When the news about him kept spreading and crowds kept coming to him after his cure of a leper, Luke describes Jesus' common custom when he writes, "He [Jesus] would withdraw to deserted places and pray" (5:16). Even in his last week in Jerusalem, he would teach every day in the Temple area and spend the night at the Mount of Olives (21:37). When he went there for his final night of prayer before his arrest, it was according to his usual practice: "He came and went, as was his custom to the Mount of Olives" (22:39).

Jesus' Prayer and Daily Decisions

Luke describes Jesus' prayer more often than any of the other Gospels. Even his childhood is described in an atmosphere of prayer and peace. The prophet Simeon came into the Temple at the time that Jesus was presented there, forty days after his birth. Simeon had been told by the Holy Spirit that he would not die until he had seen the Lord's Messiah. So he took the child Jesus in his arms and prayed to God, saying, "Master, now you are dismissing your servant in peace" (2:29). A favorite departure greeting was "Go in peace." Simeon heard the final greeting of peace from God before his death. A prophetess Anna also appeared on the scene. She spent her days in the Temple area, fasting and praying. She also recognized the child Jesus and "spoke about the child to all who were looking for the redemption of Israel" (2:38).

Only Luke notes that Jesus was praying after his baptism when the Spirit came down in the form of a dove (3:22). This serves as a model for the gospel audience in the Acts of the Apostles as the multitude of believers pray for the coming of the Spirit in the first Pentecost (1:14). Before the important selection of his twelve apostles, "he (Jesus) spent the whole night in prayer to God" (6:12). The important time for Peter's first confession of his faith came "when Jesus was praying alone, with only the disciples near him" (9:18). The transfiguration of Jesus occurs during his time of prayer on a mountaintop (9:28). At such times the power of his inner communion with God erupts and manifests itself on his face and features.

When the seventy disciples return from their journey, "Jesus rejoiced in the Holy Spirit and thanked his Father for their success" (10:21). The Lord's prayer was taught after Jesus was alone in prayer. When he had finished, his disciples came and asked him to teach them how to pray as he did (11:1-2). At the Last Supper, the conversion of Peter and the beginnings of the Church come about as a response to Jesus' prayer. Jesus said to Peter. "I have prayed for you that your own faith may not fail; and you, when once you have turned back, strengthen your brothers" (22:32). Even on the cross, Jesus' prayer for others precedes the conversion of the centurion and one of the "criminals" crucified at the same time (23:34).

THE DUPLICATION OF JESUS' PRAYER IN THE EARLY CHURCH, ESPECIALLY REGARDING PEACE

Just as Jesus prayed for the Holy Spirit at his baptism, so also the Twelve, Mary, the women, and other disciples gathered together in Jerusalem to pray before the first Pentecost: "All these devoted themselves to prayer" (Acts 1:13-14). Peace concerns oneness through breaking down divisions and this characterizes the Pentecost scene. A principal source of division is language and culture. In the Pentecost story, we find a five-fold repetition of "language," with the Greek *glossa* three times and *dialektos* twice. The crowd marvels that through the gift of the Spirit, Jews from sixteen ethnic and language areas are able to hear about God's deeds of power in their own language (2:11) .

Luke is not merely describing a linguistic phenomenon, but the oneness that results from a new spirit, charismatic language. This theme of oneness is reinforced by the fact that "they were all gathered together in *one place"* (2:1). The source of this oneness is the Spirit: Peter explains that it fulfills the prophecy of Joel: "In the last days it will be, God declares, that I will pour out my Spirit upon all flesh and your sons and daughters shall prophesy" (Joel 2:28; Acts 2:17). The fact that Joel mentions daughters as well as sons shows that the Spirit overcomes the divisions of gender. So it is significant that Luke has underlined the presence of women including the mother of Jesus (1:14).

Luke also appears to have in mind a great reversal of the story of the tower of Babel (Gen 11:1-9). It begins with the statement: "Now the whole earth had one language and the same words." So they assembled together to build a tower to the sky as a name and memorial to themselves. But God came down to see what they were doing and was displeased with their pride and effort to make unity possible by their own power alone. So God said, "Come, let us go down, and confuse their language there, so that they will not understand one another's speech" (11:7). Luke certainly knew this story and could be telling his Scripture-conscious audience that the new spirit-language of Pentecost is God's way to bring oneness and peace to the world. This would reverse the tower of Babel story.

There are several "Pentecost" stories in Acts as prayer and the Spirit break down barriers to bring together people in peace. After the Jerusalem Jewish Pentecost, there is a Jewish-Gentile Pentecost between Peter and his companions and Cornelius the Roman centurion along with his household. In reference to breaking external barriers to peace, one of the greatest was the separating wall between Jews and Gentiles, symbolized by the three-foot high barrier in the Temple court forbidding Gentiles to proceed further under pain of death. So when the centurion Cornelius and his entourage came to visit Peter and his companion Jewish Christians, this was a tremendous challenge.

Behind the event is the powerful prayer of both Peter and the centurion. This centurion "gave alms generously to the people and prayed constantly to God" (10:2). In response, in a vision, an angel told him that his prayers were answered and that he should send messengers to ask Peter to come to his home. Yet this visit in itself presented an "impossible" barrier for observing Jews who could not eat or enter a Gentile home. Later when Jewish Christians had heard of this visit, they criticized Peter saying, "Why did you go to uncircumcised men and eat with them?" (11:3). Peter had to explain that during prayer he received a triple vision-revelation that he should not regard as "unclean" (Gentiles and their food) what God had created clean (11:4-11). So Peter told them, "The Spirit told me to go to them and not to make a distinction between them and us."

After entering Cornelius's home, Peter addressed them and his own six companions appealing to the themes of peace, power, and the Holy Spirit. He told them "the message God sent to the people of Israel, preaching *peace* by Jesus Christ—he is Lord of all" (10:36). Here we find echoes of the angels' message at Jesus' birth of *peace on earth* and Jesus as *Lord* (Luke 2:11, 14). Then Peter continued, "God anointed Jesus of Nazareth with the *Holy Spirit and with power*" (Acts 10:38). As Peter spoke, "The Holy Spirit fell upon all who heard the word":

> The circumcised believers who had come with Peter were astounded that the gift of the Holy Spirit had been poured out even on the Gentiles, for they heard them speaking in *tongues* and extolling God. Then Peter said, "Can anyone withhold the water for baptizing these people who have received the Holy Spirit just as we have?" (10:45-47).

We note that Peter considers their experience to be the same that he and others had received at the first Pentecost. The specific mention of *tongues* again brings out that God has created a new language to join people together despite tremendous obstacles.

A third "Pentecost" occurs when Paul first left Europe and entered the Roman province of Asia. There he encountered disciples of John the Baptist. These people had received John's baptism but had never received the baptism of the Spirit through the resurrection of Jesus. Paul further instructed them and baptized them "in the name of the Lord Jesus" (Acts 19:10). Then Paul laid his hands on them and "the Holy Spirit came upon them, and they spoke in *tongues* and prophesied." Here again we find the charismatic gifts, notably *tongues* as a sign of the one new unifying language of the Spirit.

THE INNER POWER OF THE SPIRIT VERSUS EXTERNAL POWER, AUTHORITY, AND BARRIERS TO PEACE

"Power," *dynamis* is a favorite theme in Luke, more than any other Gospel. However the combination of power and the Holy Spirit occurs only in his Gospel and his second volume Acts of the Apostles. This combination is the direct opposite of external power and authority. We find this contrast explicitly in the Acts of the Apostles when the disciples asked the risen Jesus about the coming "promise of the Father" (1:6). They asked (in terms of earthly power), "Lord, is this the time when you will restore the kingdom to Israel?" In contrast, Jesus replied, "You will receive *power* when the *Holy Spirit* has come upon you; and you will be my witnesses in Jerusalem, in all Judea and Samaria, and to the ends of the earth" (1:8).

SPIRIT AND POWER IN JESUS

The combination of Spirit and Power is found from the gospel beginning. In contrast to the military power of King Herod of Judea (1:5), the angel Gabriel tells Zechariah that his son John will be filled with the Holy Spirit and will lead the way "with the spirit and power of Elijah" (1:17). The same angel announces to Mary that she will give birth to a child who will reign over the house of David forever, but this will come about through a hidden mysterious birth: "The *Holy Spirit* will come upon you, and the *power* of the Most High will overshadow you; therefore the child to be born will be holy; he will be called Son of God" (1:35). After his temptation in the desert, "Jesus, filled with the *power of the Holy Spirit* returned to Galilee" (4:14).

In all, "Spirit" is found twenty-seven times in Luke and sixty-five times in Acts. "Power" occurs 17 times in Luke and 18 times in Acts. At times, this Spirit and Power is not only in contrast with earthly power but in opposition and victory over the power of the devil. Thus Jesus, "filled with the power of the Spirit" is led by the spirit into the desert where he wins an anticipatory victory over the devil (4:13) that is to be completed at his death.

THE ACTS OF THE APOSTLES

In the Acts of the Apostles we find the same inner power of the Spirit connected with prayer in response to external authority. After the resurrection, when Peter and John were first arrested for teaching in the Temple area, the high priest and council questioned their authority to publicly teach. Peter, "filled with the Holy Spirit," responded that it was "in the name of Jesus Christ of Nazareth whom you crucified, whom God raised from the dead" (4:10). Attempting to prevent the spread of this teaching, the council called them and ordered them "not to speak or teach at all in the name of Jesus." Peter and John answered, "Whether it is right in God's sight to listen to you rather than to God, you must judge; for we cannot keep from speaking about what we have seen and heard" (4:19-20).

After their release Peter and John went to their friends and reported to them what the chief priests and elders had commanded them. In response they all prayed together for the strength to continue on, just as Jesus, in facing persecution from Herod and Pontius Pilate. They asked God for the ability "to speak your word with all boldness." When they finished their prayer, "the place in which they were gathered together was shaken; and they were all filled with the Holy Spirit and spoke the word of God with boldness" (4:31). This boldness, *parrēsia*, was the same characteristic that the ruling council had observed in Peter and John "when they saw the *boldness* of Peter and John and realized that they were uneducated and ordinary men, they were amazed and recognized them as companions of Jesus" (4:13). The inner power of the Holy Spirit had given them the courage to confront external power and authority in the same way that Jesus did.

As a special example, Stephen, one of the seven assistants to the Twelve, became the first martyr for the faith. Luke describes him as a man "full of faith and the Holy Spirit" (6:3). As Stephen was being stoned to death by the ruling council, he imitated the last prayer of Jesus on the cross for his enemies. Stephen knelt down and prayed, "Lord, do not hold this sin against them" (7:60). Luke immediately connects this with the young man Saul (later Paul) who "had approved of their killing them" and had guarded over the cloaks of those who executed Stephen. For Luke, it was the dying prayer of Stephen that made possible the conversion of Paul and his resulting apostolate to the Gentile world.

SUMMARY

The combat of Jesus and the early Church against external power and authority relied on the "weapons" of the power of the Holy Spirit and prayer. Luke presents John the Baptist and Jesus as practicing a desert spirituality. Yet Jesus, in contrast to John brought the desert out to the ordinary people. Both John and Jesus provided the early Church with examples and teaching on prayer they could use in situations of crisis and serious opposition. The inner power of the Spirit and prayer also enabled the Church to create harmony and peace by breaking down the barriers of language and culture through the miracle of an inner language of the spirit. This is illustrated through the series of Pentecosts in the Acts of the Apostles.

COROLLARY FOR TODAY

The message of "Peace on Earth" cannot come to the world without the inner forces of prayer and the power of the Spirit. So-called "military solutions" sometimes seem to bring outer peace and security, but it is short lasting. The ordinary person is often called upon merely to support their leaders in such an effort. However, the power of the Spirit is open to each individual and is increased in geometric progression as person joins to person in small or large groups. Peace organizations such as Pax Christi have recommended that each individual or family set aside at least five minutes each day in meditation or prayer to send vibrations of peace and nonviolence to where it is so much needed. A "desert spirituality" can be open to any person who also finds a quiet place for undisturbed prayer each day. I have been told that many of the smallest and poorest homes in India have a curtained corner where individuals can come for solitude and prayer.

A FINAL REFLECTION ON HOPE

"Turning the world upside-down" are Luke's own words from Acts 17:6. They reflect the view that God desires to turn the world upside-down by embracing a theology and praxis of peace and nonviolence. This is the upside-down view in Mary's *Magnificat* when she sings that God "has brought down the powerful from their thrones, and lifted up the lowly" (1:52). In her own case, she accepted the message of the angel Gabriel who said, "Nothing will be impossible with God" (1:37). These words could be applied to the world of today where it is easy to lose hope that the forces of peace, love, and nonviolence will prevail. Our greatest resource is faith and hope, just as it was for the mother of Jesus. Just before her *Magnificat*, Elizabeth said to Mary, "Blessed is she who believed that there would be a fulfillment of what was spoken to her by the Lord" (1:45).

Bibliography

This is not meant to be a complete bibliography of sources but a selection of those most frequently used in writing this book.

Allison, Dale C. *The Sermon on the Mount.* New York: Crossroads, 1999.

Boadt, Lawrence. *Reading the Old Testament: An Introduction.* Mahwah, N.J.: Paulist Press, 1984.

Byrne, Brendan. "Jesus as Messiah in the Gospel of Luke: Discerning a Pattern of Correction." *Catholic Biblical Quarterly* 65 (2003) 80–95.

Cassidy, Richard J. *Jesus, Politics and Society: A Study of Luke's Gospel.* Maryknoll, N.Y.: Orbis, 1978.

Cassidy, Richard J., and Philip Scharper, eds. *Political Issues in Luke–Acts.* Maryknoll, N.Y.: Orbis, 1983.

Donahue, John R. "Biblical Perspectives on Justice," in John C. Haughey, *The Faith That Does Justice.* Mahwah, N.J.: Paulist, 1977.

Doorly, William J. *Obsession with Justice: The Story of the Deuteronomists.* Mahwah, N.J.: Paulist, 1994.

Ford, J. Massyngbaerd. *My Enemy Is My Guest: Jesus and Non-Violence in Luke.* Maryknoll, N.Y.: Orbis, 1984.

Grassi, Joseph A. *The Hidden Heroes of the Gospel.* Collegeville: The Liturgical Press, 1989.

———. *Informing the Future: Social Justice and the New Testament.* Mahwah, N.J.: Paulist, 2003.

Hamilton, Jeffries M. *Social Justice and Deuteronomy: The Case of Deuteronomy 15*. Society of Biblical Literature, 1992.

Johnson, Luke T. *The Literary Function of Possessions in Luke–Acts*. Atlanta: John Knox, 1983.

Malina, Bruce. *The New Testament World: Insights from Cultural Anthropology*. Atlanta: John Knox, 1981.

Murphy, Catherine M. *The Disposition of Wealth in the Literature and Practice of the Qumran Community and Its Relevance for the Study of the New Testament*. Notre Dame, Ind.: Dept. of Theology, 1999.

Nardone, Enrique. *Los Que Buscan la Justicia: Un Estudio de la Justicia en el Mundo Biblico*. Aldecoa, S.L., Burgos, Spain: Editorial Verbo Divino, 1997.

Nolan, Albert. *Jesus before Christianity*. Maryknoll, N.Y.: Orbis, 2001.

Neyrey, Jerome. *The Passion According to Luke*. Mahwah, N.J.: Paulist, 1985.

Oakman, Douglas E. *Jesus and the Economic Questions of His Day*. Lewiston/Queenstown: Edwin Mellen Press, 1986.

Powell, Mark Allen. *What Are They Saying about Luke?* Mahwah, N.J.: Paulist, 1989.

Pleins, J. David. *The Social Vision of the Hebrew Bible*. Nashville: Westminster/John Knox, 2000.

Schochet, Elijah, Juda. *Animal Life in Jewish Traditions: Attitudes and Relationships*. New York: Ktav Publishing House, 1984.

Senior, Donald. "With 'Swords and Clubs'—The Setting of Mark's Community and His Critique of Abusive Power." *Biblical Theology Bulletin* 17 (1987) 10–20.

Topel, L. John. *Children of a Compassionate God: A Theological Exegesis of Luke 6:20-49*. Collegeville: The Liturgical Press, 2001.

Index